Poems from the Past

Active approaches to pre-twentieth-century poetry

Mary Berry and Alex Madina

CAMBRIDGE
UNIVERSITY PRESS

CAMBRIDGE UNIVERSITY PRESS
Cambridge, New York, Melbourne, Madrid, Cape Town, Singapore, São Paulo, Delhi

Cambridge University Press
The Edinburgh Building, Cambridge CB2 8RU, UK

www.cambridge.org
Information on this title: www.cambridge.org/9780521585651

First published 1997
Reprinted 1998, 2004

A catalogue record for this publication is available from the British Library

ISBN 978-0-521-58565-1 paperback

Transferred to digital printing 2008

Illustrations by Sean Creagh and Stephen Peart
Cover illustration by Sean Creagh

Acknowledgements
We are grateful to the following for permission to reproduce photographs:
The Bridgeman Art Library/Tate Gallery, London, painting: *April Love, 1855-56,* by Arthur Hughes
(1832–1915), pages 81 and 83; Bruce Coleman Collection (Kim Taylor) page 9; Robert Harding
Picture Library/Bildagentur Schuster (D Kraus), page 99; The *Illustrated London News,* engraving
from Old & New London 'Swallow Street during its demolition', pages 29 and 31; The Image Bank
(Daniel Hummel), page 19; Paul Mulcahy, pages 47, 49, 87, 89; Tony Stone Images, pages 15
(Manoj Shah), 93.

The authors and publishers would like to thank the following for permission to reproduce copyright
material:

P. 43 'Night Mail' by W.H. Auden reprinted by permission of Faber & Faber Ltd; p. 53 'The Old Men
Admiring Themselves in the Water' taken from *The Collected Poems of W.B Yeats* reprinted by
permission of A.P. Watt Ltd on behalf of Anne and Michael Yeats; p. 87 'Matilda Who Told Lies and
was Burned to Death' by Hilaire Belloc reprinted with permission from Random House UK Ltd;
P. 79 'Stopping by Woods on a Snowy Evening' from *The Poetry of Robert Frost,* edited by Edward
Connery Lathem and reprinted with permission from Random House UK Ltd.

Every effort has been made to reach copyright holders; the publishers would like to hear from
anyone whose rights they have unknowingly infringed.

CONTENTS

People and Relationships

The Ticking of Time

The Rime of the Ancient Mariner

INTRODUCTION

Almost all the poems in this book were written before the twentieth century began. The collection ranges from AD 1600 to 1900. You will already know some of the poems, and we hope you will enjoy reading some new ones.

You may find some of the words in the poems unfamiliar because the poet is trying to describe something particular or because the English language has changed. Reading the word out loud or using a dictionary may help you, and so may a little guesswork.

The poems are grouped together by theme so that you can compare how different poets deal with similar ideas and subjects. The thematic sections are in date order where possible, with the earliest poem first.

You'll notice all the poems are on the right, with the suggested activities opposite. You do not have to do all the activities: they are simply possible ways of becoming actively involved in the verse. You can work on the activities on your own or in groups. All directions, for example to group size, are simply suggestions, and should be altered to fit your needs.

We hope you will find this collection of pre-twentieth century poetry fascinating and challenging. It is intended as a beginning, to help you find some poets and poems you like so that you can go and read more on your own. As you go through the book you will find many echoes of modern life. People in the past were much like we are today: they too enjoyed ghost stories, arguments and interesting descriptions of daily life.

Have a good read.

Mary Berry and Alex Madina

STRANGE WORLDS

1 Witches on Stage (groups of three or more)

Work out an effective dramatisation of the witches' lines. If you work in a group larger than three, share out the lines so that everyone speaks. Several voices chanting together can add to the dramatic effect, as can movement, storm, sound effects and music.

2 The Evil Charm Book (individual or in pairs)

Imagine that one of these witches goes home to write the charm down in her spell book. She would probably start by naming the spell and explaining its effect. Then she would list the ingredients, draw them, say where they could be found and how they could be cooked. Write and illustrate the spell. You may find the glossary below helpful:

'blind-worm'	slow-worm, believed then to be an eyeless, poisonous worm
'howlet'	young owl
'mummy'	mummified corpse
'hemlock'	poisonous plant – if dug up at night it was believed to be more deadly
'drab'	prostitute
'tiger's chawdron'	tiger's entrails

3 The Observer

Plan and write the story of a character who hid and watched the witches on that night. Develop this plan as a starting point:

Who the observer is
What I was doing there...

Witches' actions
I saw them...
I heard them...

Place
It was...

WHAT THE OBSERVER SAW

Witches' appearance
I saw three hags...

The night and the atmosphere
I saw black thunderous clouds..
I felt...

The Witches' Chant from *Macbeth*

Thunder. Enter the three WITCHES

FIRST WITCH	Thrice the brindled cat hath mewed.
SECOND WITCH	Thrice and once the hedge-pig whined.
THIRD WITCH	Harpier cries, ''Tis time, 'tis time.'
FIRST WITCH	Round about the cauldron go;
	In the poisoned entrails throw. 5
	Toad, that under cold stone
	Days and nights has thirty-one
	Sweltered venom sleeping got,
	Boil thou first i' th' charmèd pot.
ALL	Double, double toil and trouble; 10
	Fire burn, and cauldron bubble.
SECOND WITCH	Fillet of a fenny snake,
	In the cauldron boil and bake:
	Eye of newt, and toe of frog,
	Wool of bat, and tongue of dog, 15
	Adder's fork, and blind-worm's sting,
	Lizard's leg, and howlet's wing,
	For a charm of powerful trouble,
	Like a hell-broth, boil and bubble.
ALL	Double, double toil and trouble, 20
	Fire burn, and cauldron bubble.
THIRD WITCH	Scale of dragon, tooth of wolf,
	Witches' mummy, maw and gulf
	Of the ravined salt-sea shark,
	Root of hemlock, digged i' th' dark; 25
	Liver of blaspheming Jew,
	Gall of goat, and slips of yew,
	Slivered in the moon's eclipse;
	Nose of Turk, and Tartar's lips,
	Finger of birth-strangled babe, 30
	Ditch-delivered by a drab,
	Make the gruel thick and slab.
	Add thereto a tiger's chawdron
	For th' ingredience of our cauldron.
ALL	Double, double toil and trouble, 35
	Fire burn, and cauldron bubble.
SECOND WITCH	Cool it with a baboon's blood,
	Then the charm is firm and good.

William Shakespeare

1 The Storytellers (pairs)

Read the poem aloud to one another several times and in several ways.

- Change readers at each punctuation mark.
- Chant it like a spell. Vary your speed and tone of voice.
- Say the last line angrily as you realise an ingredient is missing.

2 The Witches' Intentions (groups of four)

Clues in the poem hint at the reason for the witches' charm. They have dug a hole with their fingernails and have made wax and wool 'pictures' (models or effigies) of their victims. What do they want the needles for? Why bury them?

Note down why you think the witches are making this charm. List each ingredient and state what you imagine its purpose to be.

3 Descriptive Writing (pairs)

This poem is very detailed in its description of sights and sounds. For example, Jonson refers to the sounds of 'timbrels' (tambourines), dogs baying (howling) and the sight of a vivid red 'burning' sky. Jot down all the descriptive phrases in the poem, and add touches of your own detail to each of these.

Use these notes as a basis for a piece of detailed descriptive writing. Here is one student's opening:

The owl flew silently across the night sky. In this intense blackness only the creatures of the night dared go abroad. The winged, silent bat swooped low, the toad croaked his lonely song.

4 Rhythm (pairs)

Poetry can be written in many different rhythms. Read 'The Witches' Charm' aloud and try to hear, or tap out, the rhythm. How many syllables are there in each line?

Where does Jonson change the rhythm? Why?

The Witches' Charm

The owl is abroad, the bat, and the toad,
    And so is the cat-a-mountain;
The ant and the mole sit both in a hole,
    And frog peeps out o' the fountain;
The dogs they do bay, and the timbrels play,
    The spindle is now a-turning;
The moon it is red, and the stars are fled,
    But all the sky is a-burning:
The ditch is made, and our nails the spade,
With pictures full, of wax and of wool;
Their livers I stick with needles quick:
There lacks but the blood to make up the flood.

Ben Jonson

1 The Hag (groups of four)

The poem describes a witch's flight over land and sea. It uses rhythm and rhyme to create pace and excitement. Work out a dramatic reading using all four voices. Is the pace faster at certain moments? Should the volume of your reading vary?

2 Working out Rhyme Schemes (pairs)

Poets sometimes rhyme words at the ends of lines to give structure to their poems. The rhyming lines link to make a rhyme scheme. This can be shown in note form by using letters to represent each new rhyme. Line 1 of 'The Hag' ends with the word 'astride', and as it is the first line of the poem call it (a). 'Astride' rhymes with 'ride' so this will also be (a). 'Together' (line 3) does not rhyme with what has gone before, so it is labelled (b). Which is the next (b) rhyme?

Here is the rhyme scheme for the first four lines of verse 1. Can you finish it?

The Hag is astride,	(a)
This night for to ride;	(a)
The Devil and she together:	(b)
Through thick, and through thin,	(c)

What is the rhyme scheme of 'A Charm, or An Allay for Love'? Why do you think these poems rhyme?

3 The Rest of the Rhyming Ride (pairs)

Imagine the witch rides home by a different route. Describe what she does on her way, the people she flies over and the places she passes. Use the plan below to start your work.

What she does	People she flies over	Places she passes
steals milk to drink	descends over dreaming heads	past shop, past spire

Use your chart to write more verses of 'The Hag'. Try to use the same rhyme scheme and rhythm as Herrick's.

The Hag

The Hag is astride,
This night for to ride;
The Devil and she together:
Through thick, and through thin,
Now out, and then in,   5
Though ne'er so foul be the weather.

A Thorn or a Burr
She takes for a Spur:
With a lash of a Bramble she rides now,
Through Brakes and through Briars,   10
O'er Ditches, and Mires,
She follows the Spirit that guides now.

No Beast, for his food,
Dares now range the wood;
But hush't in his lair he lies lurking: 15
While mischiefs, by these,
On Land and on Seas,
At noon of Night are a working.

The storm will arise,
And trouble the skies;   20
This night, and more for the wonder,
The ghost from the Tomb
Affrighted shall come,
Called out by the clap of the Thunder.

Robert Herrick

A Charm, or An Allay for Love

If so be a Toad be laid
In a Sheeps-skin newly flayed,
And that tied to man 'twill sever
Him and his affections ever.

Robert Herrick

1 Ghostbusters (groups of three or four)

There are many stories about ghosts and poltergeists who are not at peace because of something that happened while they were alive.

One of you lives in a haunted house. You call in a company which claims to be able to rid all houses of troublesome ghosts. Improvise the scene from the moment the ghost removal company arrives.

2 Ghost With a Regional Accent (pairs)

There are hints in 'The Ghost's Song' that the speaker has a regional accent. Where does the ghost come from?

Present a reading of the poem in your choice of regional accent. At the end of your reading be prepared to explain your choice of accent by quoting words which you feel are regional.

3 A Ghost has a Say

The unhappy ghost exclaims 'Wae's me! wae's me!' (woe is me). Note down the reasons for the ghost's sorrow.

Write an explanation of 'The Ghost's Song' in three paragraphs:

- One – title of the poem, who wrote it, who is the speaker in the poem, what the poem is about.
- Two – the language of the poem: the regional words, the rhymes used and their effect, the repetition used and its effect. Is it, as the title suggests, a song? What is the mood of the poem?
- Three – your opinion of the poem.

4 Good Wishes Then, and Now (pairs)

The powerful chant in 'Good Wish' is said to a child to bring good luck in the future. Talk about what 'good wishes' are being sent to the child – for example, might 'Power of eagle' be the strength and majesty to soar above problems?

Choose two or three wishes and explain them. What good things would you wish for yourself?

The Ghost's Song

Wae's me! wae's me!
The acorn's not yet
Fallen from the tree
That's to grow the wood,
That's to make the cradle,
That's to rock the bairn,
That's to grow a man,
That's to lay me.

Anon

Good Wish

Power of raven be thine,
Power of eagle be thine,
    Power of the Fiann.

Power of storm be thine,
Power of moon be thine,   5
    Power of sun.

Power of sea be thine,
Power of land be thine,
    Power of heaven.

Goodness of sea be thine,   10
Goodness of earth be thine,
    Goodness of heaven.

Each day be joyous to thee,
No day be grievous to thee,
    Honour and compassion.   15

Love of each face be thine,
Death on the pillow be thine,
    Thy Saviour's presence.

Anon: translated from the Gaelic
by Alexander Carmichael

1 Resentment and Anger Grow and Grow (groups of four)

Things people do or say can be really annoying. Rather than confronting them with your feelings you might keep quiet, a bit like this:

Improvise a situation where you felt annoyed with someone but didn't say anything. Did this make your resentment worse?

2 Opening Lines (pairs)

Present the opening verse of 'A Poison Tree' using Blake's words, drama and *tableaux* (freeze at important words to show the action).
Then explain in two clear sentences what you think Blake is saying.
Do you think he's right?

3 Metaphors (pairs)

'A Poison Tree' uses an *extended metaphor* to compare increasing anger to a poisonous tree growing. Create a series of pictures with captions which explain the metaphor.

I'm angry with my enemy. But I dont say anything.

The seed of anger (wrath) grows into a small tree.

Is 'The Tiger' about a real tiger or is this poem metaphorical?

4 The Definite Article or the Indefinite? (pairs)

In English grammar, the word 'the' is called the definite article. 'The chair' means a specific chair – definitely that chair and no other. 'A chair' refers to any chair. What do the titles 'The Tiger' and 'A Poison Tree' suggest?

The Tiger

Tiger, tiger, burning bright,
In the forests of the night:
What immortal hand or eye
Could frame thy fearful symmetry?

In what distant deeps or skies,   5
Burnt the fire of thine eyes?
On what wings dare he aspire?
What the hand dare seize the fire?

And what shoulder, and what art,
Could twist the sinews of thy heart?   10
And when thy heart began to beat,
What dread hand? and what dread feet?

What the hammer? what the chain?
In what furnace was thy brain?
What the anvil? what dread grasp   15
Dare its deadly terrors clasp?

When the stars threw down their spears,
And watered Heaven with their tears,
Did he smile his work to see?
Did he who made the lamb make thee?   20

Tiger, tiger, burning bright,
In the forests of the night:
What immortal hand or eye
Dare frame thy fearful symmetry?

William Blake

A Poison Tree

I was angry with my friend;
I told my wrath – my wrath did end.
I was angry with my foe;
I told it not – my wrath did grow.

And I watered it in fears,   5
Night and morning with my tears,
And I sunnèd it with smiles,
And with soft deceitful wiles.

And it grew both day and night,
Till it bore an apple bright.   10
And my foe beheld it shine,
And he knew that it was mine,

And into my garden stole
When the night had veiled the pole.
In the morning glad I see   15
My foe outstretched beneath the tree.

William Blake

1 An Island Moves (pairs or groups of three)

In the Middle Ages, stories were told about a huge sea monster called the Kraken. It was so big that people mistook its back for an island. One group of sailors is said to have climbed on to the back of the Kraken while it was asleep, waking it up by accident when they lit cooking fires.

Imagine you are the surviving sailors. Improvise your story of the island visit. Write your account as a story or sensational newspaper piece.

2 Radio Kraken (groups of three or four)

Tennyson gives a detailed description of the Kraken sleeping deep in the dark recesses of the sea bed. Use the poem to prepare a radio programme for primary children on the subject of the Kraken. You might include:

- factual information about the monster (look in a dictionary of myths)
- a dramatic reading of Tennyson's poem set to music
- Tennyson discussing how he presented the creature
- children imagining the Kraken and the huge 'polypi' (cuttlefish) which 'winnow' (sift or fan) their way through the green water.

3 Phoenix and Kraken (pairs)

The Phoenix was a mythical bird. Stories are told of it living for over five hundred years, then flying onto a funeral pyre to burn to death. It rose from the ashes to live again. How is Tennyson's Kraken different from the Phoenix?

4 The Children's Illustrated Kraken (pairs or groups of three)

Write a chapter of a poetry book for 6 to 8 year-olds. On one page write a few lines of verse and illustrate it; on the opposite page explain what it means. A double page might look something like this:

The Kraken

Below the thunders of the upper deep;
Far, far beneath in the abysmal sea,
His ancient, dreamless, uninvaded sleep
The Kraken sleepeth: faintest sunlights flee
About his shadowy sides: above him swell
Huge sponges of millennial growth and height;
And far away into the sickly light,
From many a wondrous grot and secret cell
Unnumber'd and enormous polypi
Winnow with giant arms the slumbering green.
There hath he lain for ages and will lie
Battening upon huge seaworms in his sleep,
Until the latter fire shall heat the deep;
Then once by man and angels to be seen,
In roaring he shall rise and on the surface die.

Alfred, Lord Tennyson

1 Myth

Myths describe how the normally silent swan sings as it dies. The sound is rarely heard, and it is said to be magnificent and frightening.

- How is the sound shown to be magnificent in Tennyson's poem?
- What suggests that it is also terrifying?

2 Oxymoron (pairs)

Lines 21–30 of 'The Dying Swan' describe the swan's death song. Read these lines and find where Tennyson uses an *oxymoron* (two opposite words, one after the other). Write down these two words and explain why Tennyson uses the oxymoron.

3 What You Expect from Song (groups of three)

In describing the swan's death song, Tennyson uses poetic techniques to make the language sound flowing, song-like and mysterious. The spider diagram below shows some of the techniques. See if you can add to it.

Alliteration (see page 20)
Examples: 'the river ran'

What this does: the sound of the repeated 'r' makes the line and sound flow like w_____.

Open rhymes (using vowels)
Examples:

What this does:

TECHNIQUES TO MAKE THE POEM SONG-LIKE

Repetition
Examples:

What this does:

Simile
Examples: In lines 28–35

What this does: the swan's death song is compared with ..

The Dying Swan

1

The plain was grassy, wild and bare,
Wide, wild, and open to the air,
Which had built up everywhere
   An under-roof of doleful gray.
With an inner voice the river ran,   5
Adown it floated a dying swan,
     And loudly did lament.
  It was the middle of the day.
Ever the weary wind went on.
     And took the reed-tops as it went.   10

2

Some blue peaks in the distance rose,
And white against the cold-white sky,
Shone out their crowning snows.
  One willow over the river wept,
And shook the wave as the wind did sigh;   15
Above in the wind was the swallow,
    Chasing itself at its own wild will,
    And far thro' the marish green and still
    The tangled water-courses slept,
Shot over with purple, and green, and yellow.   20

3

The wild swan's death-hymn took the soul
Of that waste place with joy
Hidden in sorrow: at first to the ear
The warble was low, and full and clear;
And floating about the under-sky,   25
Prevailing in weakness, the coronach stole
Sometimes afar, and sometimes anear;
But anon her awful jubilant voice,
With a music strange and manifold,
Flow'd forth on a carol free and bold;   30
As when a mighty people rejoice
With shawms, and with cymbals, and harps of gold,
And the tumult of their acclaim is roll'd
Thro' the open gates of the city afar,
To the shepherd who watcheth the evening star.   35
And the creeping mosses and clambering weeds,
And the willow-branches hoar and dank,
And the wavy swell of the soughing reeds,
And the wave-worn horns of the echoing bank,
And the silvery marish-flowers that throng   40
The desolate creeks and pools among,
Were flooded over with eddying song.

Alfred, Lord Tennyson

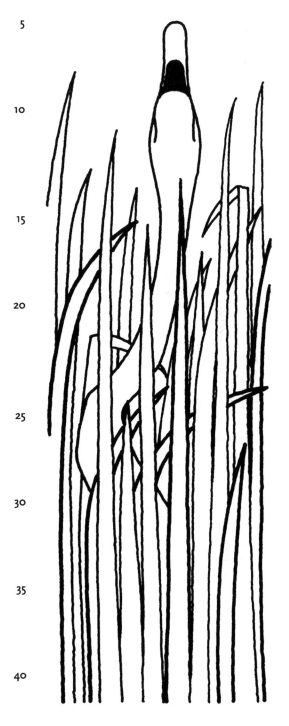

1 Raw to Cooked (pairs)

All you will get here are the raw 'ingredients' of a poem: the ideas, the form and the techniques that a famous poet used. Mix the ingredients together and 'cook' your own version of the poem.

Follow the clues one at a time and write the poem yourself. Use a large sheet of paper to draft your ideas.

CLUE 1
Title: the poem is called 'The Eagle'.

CLUE 2
Structure: the poem is divided into two three-line verses, or stanzas. Draw lines on your paper ready for the poem.

CLUE 3
Line 1: the eagle grips hold of the rock. The poem describes his talons focusing on the shape of them. The line begins:

He clasps   .   .   .   .   .   .

The poet uses *alliteration* (repetition of a consonant) in this line to stress just how tightly the eagle holds on to the mountain.

CLUE 4
The poet also uses *metre*. This poem has a regular beat, or rhythm. The first line has eight syllables arranged in an alternate unstressed (ᴗ) and stressed (/) pattern. Go back to your first line and see if you can rework it as an eight-syllable line with a pattern:

   ᴗ   /   ᴗ   /   ᴗ   /   ᴗ   /
He clasps   .   .   .   .

CLUE 5
Line 2: this describes how high the eagle flies and how near the sun. It also describes his isolation.

CLUE 6
Line 3: this describes the eagle perched high on his crag surrounded by vivid blue sky. The last word of this line rhymes with the last word of line 1.

CLUE 7
Verse 2 uses the same metre. The first line describes what is beneath the eagle. The picture on the opposite page will help you.

CLUE 8
Line 2 describes the eagle looking out over this view. It tells us where he is.

CLUE 9

Line 3: the eagle suddenly plunges to catch his prey. The last line uses *simile* to compare his sudden swift dive to something else. The line begins:

And like . . . . .

Check your draft. Read it aloud in your group. You might use choric reading (all reading together), echo effects, or give different lines to each reader to make the reading really effective.

Tennyson and You

(a) Write up your version of 'The Eagle' and illustrate it. Look up the original poem in the library. It is called 'The Eagle' by Alfred, Lord Tennyson.

(b) Write a paragraph comparing your poem with Tennyson's.

1 Questions and Answers (pairs)

'What is Pink?' is a series of questions and answers. Read it aloud with one of you posing the questions and the other responding. Then change roles.

2 What is a Poem? (pairs)

Rossetti's poem seems simple, but it has a form, rhyme scheme and a deliberate twist at the end. Good poetry is planned and drafted. Write your own 'What is' poem using the same structure, rhyme scheme and idea as Rossetti.

(a) PLANNING

Complete a planning chart similar to the one below in which you decide what colours you want to write about, and describe them.

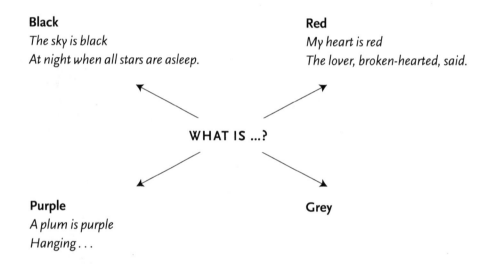

Black
The sky is black
At night when all stars are asleep.

Red
My heart is red
The lover, broken-hearted, said.

WHAT IS ...?

Purple
A plum is purple
Hanging . . .

Grey

(b) DRAFTING

Look carefully at the structure of Rossetti's poem If you count the number of syllables you'll notice she doesn't waste words. Make a list of five key things about the form of the poem you need to copy. Here's a start:

> **Rossetti's structure:**
> 1 *Lines 1, 3, 5 . . . begin with . . .*
> 2 *The rhyme scheme is . . .*
> 3 *The line lengths . . .*
> 4 *In each answer the colour is placed . . .*
> 5 *At the end of the poem . . .*

Use your plan and notes to start drafting your poem.

What is Pink?

What is pink? a rose is pink
By the fountain's brink.
What is red? a poppy's red
In its barley bed.
What is blue? the sky is blue
Where the clouds float through.
What is white? a swan is white
Sailing in the light.
What is yellow? pears are yellow,
Rich and ripe and mellow.
What is green? the grass is green,
With small flowers between.
What is violet? clouds are violet
In the summer twilight.
What is orange? why, an orange,
Just an orange!

Christina Rossetti

1 What's Galumphing On? (pairs)

Read the poem using two voices, one as narrator and the other as the character encouraging his 'son'. Discuss what you think the poem is about.

2 What Bits are English? (groups of three)

Lewis Carroll uses a mixture of real English words and made-up words to create a poem which allows you to imagine the action. The words he invents are *onomatopoeic* – they sound like the thing they represent. Which words are made up in lines 14–16 and what do they mean?

3 The Slitherhiss Slips and Snaks (groups of three)

Carroll invents a monster and then a story of how it is defeated. Invent your own 'Jabberwock' and tell its story. The following ideas may help:

(a) INVENTING A MONSTER
Select a threatening name. Carroll's monster sounds as if it jabs and strikes at you! Think about hissing or sharp-sounding words.

(b) INVENTING A LOCATION
Carroll's battle takes place in a dark wood.

- Think about a good location for your battle: a dungeon, a bleak mountain top, caverns . . .
- Invent *adjectives* (describing words) to give an impression of the place. Think about the sound of your words – *alliterative* description works well: 'dank and droopening dungeon'.

(c) INVENTING VERBS
Carroll invents *verbs* (action words) describing how the 'Jabberwock' attacks.

(d) SKETCH A PLOT
Create an illustrated plan similar to this example:

The Snatchcrak flies over the land

Armed with his swizzing sword he . . .

He steals the melificent Princess Pricenessy

To the drugeon lair goes he

To the rescue goes young Helalad

Jabberwocky

'Twas brillig, and the slithy toves
   Did gyre and gimble in the wabe;
All mimsy were the borogoves,
   And the mome raths outgrabe.

'Beware the Jabberwock, my son!   5
   The jaws that bite, the claws that catch!
Beware the Jubjub bird, and shun
   The frumious Bandersnatch!'

He took his vorpal sword in hand:
   Long time the manxome foe he sought   10
So rested he by the Tumtum tree,
   And stood awhile in thought.

And as in uffish thought he stood,
   The Jabberwock, with eyes of flame,
Came whiffling through the tulgey wood,   15
   And burbled as it came!

One, two! One, two! And through and through
   The vorpal blade went snicker-snack!
He left it dead, and with its head
   He went galumphing back.   20

'And hast thou slain the Jabberwock?
   Come to my arms, my beamish boy!
O frabjous day! Callooh! Callay!'
   He chortled in his joy.

'Twas brillig, and the slithy toves   25
   Did gyre and gimble in the wabe;
All mimsy were the borogoves,
   And the mome raths outgrabe.

Lewis Carroll

PLACES AND SEASONS

1 Onomatopoeic Reading (groups of four)

The sound of a word sometimes echoes the sound it describes. This feature of speech or writing is called *onomatopoeia*. For example, in the sentence:

'The *rustling* of leaves'

'rustling' is onomatopoeic because it echoes the sound described. As the title suggests, John Clare's 'Pleasant Sounds' is a poem about sound.

Read the poem and pick out the onomatopoeic words. Prepare a reading emphasising Clare's use of sound.

2 Onomatopoeic Pictures (pairs)

Use this chart as a basis for gathering onomatopoeic words and phrases:

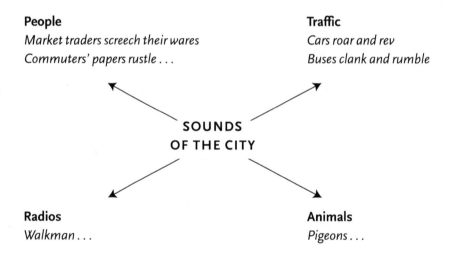

People
Market traders screech their wares
Commuters' papers rustle . . .

Traffic
Cars roar and rev
Buses clank and rumble

SOUNDS OF THE CITY

Radios
Walkman . . .

Animals
Pigeons . . .

Use your chart to write an onomatopoeic poem of your own.

3 Onomatopoeia Explained

Explain what onomatopoeia is and how it works. Support your explanation with examples from your own and Clare's poetry.

Pleasant Sounds

The rustling of leaves under the feet in
    woods and under hedges;
The crumping of cat-ice and snow down
    wood-rides, narrow lanes, and every street
    causeway;
Rustling through a wood or rather rushing,
    while the wind halloos in the oak-top like
    thunder;
The rustle of birds' wings startled from their
    nests or flying unseen into the bushes;
The whizzing of larger birds overhead in a
    wood, such as crows, puddocks,
    buzzards;
The trample of robins and woodlarks on the
    brown leaves, and the patter of squirrels
    on the green moss;
The fall of an acorn on the ground, the
    pattering of nuts on the hazel branches as
    they fall from ripeness;
The flirt of the groundlark's wing from the
    stubbles – how sweet such pictures on
    dewy mornings, when the dew flashes
    from its brown feathers!

John Clare

1 Happy New Year, Grumpy New Year (pairs)

January is the start of a new year, a fresh bright future. In 'January, 1795',
Mary Robinson shows a darker side to life.

Imagine one of you is an optimist, looking forward to a pleasant new year.
The other is a pessimist who sees misery everywhere. Read the poem and
then write down a list of the opposites it presents, for example:

> *Getting rich / People begging in the streets*

Use your list to perform a dialogue or drama in which the optimist imagines
a happy new year and the pessimist a grim one.

2 Couplets Presented and Written (pairs)

'January, 1795' is written in rhyming couplets. Each pair of lines rhymes:

> Titled gluttons dainties *carving,*
> Genius in a garret *starving.*

Couplets like this show opposites.

titled glutton carving dainties

genius in a garret . . . starving

January, 1795

Pavement slippery, people sneezing,
Lords in ermine, beggars freezing;
Titled gluttons dainties carving,
Genius in a garret starving.

Lofty mansions, warm and spacious;   5
Courtiers cringing and voracious;
Misers scarce the wretched heeding;
Gallant soldiers fighting, bleeding.

Wives who laugh at passive spouses;
Theatres, and meeting-houses;   10
Balls, where simpering misses languish;
Hospitals, and groans of anguish.

Arts and sciences bewailing;
Commerce drooping, credit failing;
Placemen mocking subjects loyal;   15
Separations, weddings royal.

Authors who can't earn a dinner;
Many a subtle rogue a winner;
Fugitives for shelter seeking;
Misers hoarding, tradesmen breaking.   20

CONTINUED ☞

3 Hear it, Beat it, See it (groups of three or four)

Each group should read the poem aloud three times. Try switching the reader every two lines. Hand on the reading at each punctuation mark. Then choose *one* of the following:

- Prepare a reading of one verse to emphasise the rhythm.
- Present two verses to the class. Try to learn the lines, act out the events or use *tableaux* (frozen moments) to show what is happening. You might add sections of your own speech or music to bring the poem to life.

Choose several opposite couplets or lines you like. Write a protest booklet, or poster campaign, pointing out the injustice of these contrasts.

4 January Now

Mary Robinson writes of the chance of peace being 'retarded' or delayed (line 43). War and peace were very significant and immediate issues in England in 1795. Find out why.

Are things better today than in January 1795? Find words or phrases which could link to something happening in the world today. Write them down. Be prepared to explain your choice to the class.

5 Criticism in 1795 (pairs)

Note down at least eight criticisms Mary Robinson makes of life in 1795. For example:

- Lines 41–42   *Cheats and scoundrels lie without blushing whilst decent men . . .*

Use these notes to write an essay about Mary Robinson's presentation of life in 1795.

January, 1795 (continued)

Taste and talents quite deserted;
All the laws of truth perverted;
Arrogance o'er merit soaring;
Merit silently deploring.

Ladies gambling night and morning;   25
Fools the works of genius scorning;
Ancient dames for girls mistake,
Youthful damsels quite forsaken.

Some in luxury delighting;
More in talking than in fighting;   30
Lovers old, and beaux decrepit;
Lordlings empty and insipid.

Poets, painters, and musicians;
Lawyers, doctors, politicians:
Pamphlets, newspaper, and odes,   35
Seeking fame by different roads.

Gallant souls with empty purses,
Generals only fit for nurses;
School-boys, smit with martial spirit,
Taking place of veteran merit.   40

Honest men can't get places,
Knaves who show unblushing faces;
Ruin hastened, peace retarded;
Candour spurned, and art rewarded.

Mary Robinson

1 Dramatic Reading (groups of four)

Prepare a dramatic reading of *one* of the poems opposite.

- For 'November' vary the tone, pace, and speaker. You may decide to add sound effects to create atmosphere.
- For 'The Months' change reader to describe each month. Try to show the *enjambement* (the way some lines flow into the next without punctuation – see page 40).

After you have heard the readings, write a paragraph on what the two poems describe. Are they similar, or different?

2 A Positive Alternative

Thomas Hood's poem depends on the negative 'No' at the beginning of the word 'November'.

Choose another month and list its good points. You may want to use the table below to help you.

APRIL
Events
A perfect chick, new hatched
Sights
A pretty, yellow flower in the hedge . . .
Feelings
A pure, smiling face . . .

Use the notes you have made to write a poem of your own. Try to use Hood's technique of linking the opening of each line to the name of the month. You could write about 'May', or about a different subject.

3 Agony Aunt Letters (two pairs)

Imagine that Thomas Hood is so depressed about November that he has written to a problem page in a magazine. In pairs discuss, plan and write Hood's letter.

When you have finished, swap your letter with another pair and write a reply suggesting what he can do and why he shouldn't be so depressed.

November

No sun, no moon,
No morn, no noon,
No dawn, no dusk, no proper time of day;
No sky, no earthly view,
No distance looking blue.   5

No road, no street, no t'other side the way;
No end to any row,
No indications where the crescents go,
No top to any steeple,
No recognition of familiar people,   10
No courtesies for showing them,
No knowing them,
No travelling at all, no locomotion,
No inkling of the way, no notion,
No go by land or ocean,   15
No mail, no post,
No news from any foreign coast,
No park, no ring, no afternoon gentility,
No company, no nobility.

No warmth, no cheerfulness, no healthful ease, 20
No comfortable feel in any member,
No shade, no shine, no butterflies, no bees,
No fruits, no flowers, no leaves, no trees:
November!

Thomas Hood

The Months

January cold desolate;
February all dripping wet;
March wind ranges;
April changes;
Birds sing in tune   5
To flowers of May,
And sunny June
Brings longest day;
In scorched July
The storm-clouds fly   10
Lightning-torn
August bears corn.
September fruit;
In rough October
Earth must disrobe her;   15
Stars fall and shoot
In keen November;
And night is long
And cold is strong
In bleak December.   20

Christina Rossetti

1 What Picture of a Winter Night? (pairs)

In just fourteen lines William Barnes describes the place, weather, atmosphere and his feelings. Draw the scene on a large sheet of paper. Label it with words or phrases from the poem. Be as accurate as you can – the churchtower is *not* brick or stone!

2 Pictures in Words (pairs)

Writers use *imagery*, or words that create pictures. Imagery helps us see or feel a scene or emotion.

Read the second verse aloud. Is something really happening? Quickly sketch the image Barnes uses in this verse, then write a brief explanation of the image and his feelings.

3 Loneliness

Have you ever felt lonely? Think back to a time when you were. Imagine the time, the place and your feelings.

Draw a spider diagram. Fill it with details of a time when you felt lonely.

Sights and sounds
Noises
Things I saw
Nature / other people?

Place
Where?
What was it like?
Colours, smells, atmosphere

LONELINESS

Time
Day / night / season
How do you know?

Feelings
It feels like . . .

Use your plan to write a poem or story about a time when you felt lonely.

A Winter Night

It was a chilly winter's night;
   And frost was glittering on the ground,
And evening stars were twinkling bright;
   And from the gloomy plain around
      Came no sóund,
But where, within the wood-girt tower,
The churchbell slowly struck the hour;

As if that all of human birth
   Had risen to the final day,
And soaring from the worn-out earth
   Were called in hurry and dismay,
      Far away;
And I alone of all mankind
Were left in loneliness behind.

William Barnes

1 Presenting For Those Who Don't Know (groups of eight)

Emily Brontë's writing contains many references to the wild and changeable Yorkshire moors where she lived.

Divide into two groups of four.

Group A: Prepare a reading and explanation of 'Spellbound'.
Group B: Prepare a reading and explanation of 'High Waving Heather'.

The reading: Each group should consider the mood of the speaker and vary the pace and tone where appropriate.
The explanation: Focus on what the poem is about and how it works. Remember that the people listening have not analysed the poem, so make your presentation as clear as possible.

At the end of the presentations write a paragraph about the poem you did *not* prepare. This tests your skills as a speaker and listener.

2 Descriptive Writing (individual or pairs)

The two scenes that Brontë describes are different: one is set at nightfall, snowfilled and surrounded by clouds; the other at midnight, and stormy. This table shows how to write vivid descriptions of the scenes by basing your ideas on words and phrases from the poems.

'Spellbound'	'High Waving Heather'
Time of day *close surrounding darkness*	**Time of day** *moonlight, bright shining stars*
I see *giant trees . . .*	**I see** *purple headed heather . . .*
I hear *wild winds . . .*	**I hear** *wind roaring like . . .*
I feel *spellbound as if . . .*	**I feel** *desolate and lonely . . .*

Use the table to draft two pieces of contrasting descriptive writing.

Spellbound

The night is darkening round me,
The wild winds coldly blow;
But a tyrant spell has bound me
And I cannot, cannot go.

The giant trees are bending
Their bare boughs weighed with snow.
And the storm is fast descending,
And yet I cannot go.

Clouds beyond clouds above me,
Wastes beyond wastes below;
But nothing drear can move me;
I will not, cannot go.

Emily Brontë

High Waving Heather

High waving heather 'neath stormy blasts bending,
Midnight and moonlight and bright shining stars,
Darkness and glory rejoicingly blending,
Earth rising to heaven and heaven descending,
Man's spirit away from its drear dungeon sending,   5
Bursting the fetters and breaking the bars.

All down the mountain sides wild forests lending
One mighty voice to the life-giving wind,
Rivers their banks in the jubilee rending,
Fast through the valleys a reckless course wending,   10
Wider and deeper their waters extending,
Leaving a desolate desert behind.

Shining and lowering and swelling and dying,
Changing forever from midnight to noon;
Roaring like thunder, like soft music sighing,   15
Shadows on shadows advancing and flying,
Lightning-bright flashes the deep gloom defying,
Coming as swiftly and fading as soon.

Emily Brontë

1 Weird Punctuation (groupwork)

Emily Dickinson describes the wind as a restless, moving visitor in her house. Notice how she uses hyphens (dashes) as the only form of punctuation and how capital letters are dotted about the poem. Robert Southey is more conventional in his use of punctuation.

- Present group readings of 'The Wind Tapped Like a Tired Man' and 'December', emphasising the different forms of punctuation in the poems.
- Write a paragraph on what you think are the effects of Dickinson's unusual punctuation.

2 Personification (pairs)

When a speaker or writer refers to an object or thing as if it is human it is called *personification*.

(a) These illustrations explain how Dickinson compares the wind to a weary man, and Southey pictures winter with a rough beard.

'The Wind – tapped like a tired Man'

'Old Winter, with a rugged beard as grey As the long moss upon the apple-tree'

Draw more illustrations which show how Dickinson or Southey personify the wind or winter.

(b) Write a paragraph which explains how each of these poems uses personification.

The Wind Tapped Like a Tired Man

The Wind – tapped like a tired Man –
And like a Host – 'Come In'
I boldly answered – entered then
My residence within

A rapid – footless Guest –   **5**
To offer whom a Chair
Were as impossible as hand
A Sofa to the Air –

No Bone had He to bind Him –
His Speech was like the Push   **10**
Of numerous Humming Birds at once
From a superior Bush –

His countenance – a Billow –
His Fingers, as He passed
Let go a music – as of tunes   **15**
Blown tremulous in Glass –

He visited – still flitting –
Then like a timid Man
Again, He tapped – 'twas flurriedly –
And I became alone –   **20**

Emily Dickinson

December

A wrinkled, crabbèd man they picture thee,
Old Winter, with a rugged beard as grey
As the long moss upon the apple-tree;
Blue-lipped, an ice-drop at thy sharp blue nose,
Close muffled up, and on thy dreary way
Plodding along through sleet and drifting snows.

They should have drawn thee by thy high-heaped hearth,
Old Winter! seated in thy great armed chair;
Watching the children at their Christmas mirth; –
Or circled by them as thy lips declare
Some merry jest, or tale of murder dire,
Or troubled spirit that disturbs the night;
Pausing at times to rouse the smouldering fire,
Or taste the old October brown and bright.

Robert Southey

1 What is 'It'? (pairs)

Emily Dickinson doesn't identify the 'It' in the title. Instead she leaves the reader clues to work out an answer.

(a) Talk about what you think 'It' is. Write your answer, adding evidence from the poem to support your opinion. The following may help:

'supercilious'	superior
'shanties'	shacks, huts
'quarry'	prey, or a place where stone is mined and cut
'pare'	shave, cut through
'Boanerges'	Sons of Thunder, thunderous sound
'omnipotent'	all-powerful

(b) An *extended metaphor* is a comparison between two things continued over several lines. What metaphor does Dickinson use? What is the effect of using this extended metaphor?

2 Enjambement (pairs)

Enjambement, or run-on lines, is when one line runs into another without being broken by punctuation.

Read the poem aloud, changing reader at each punctuation mark. When does Dickinson use enjambment? What is the effect?

3 Similar To, or Different From (groups of three)

Read 'Night Mail' and 'From a Railway Carriage' (page 43) and take notes on how Dickinson's poem differs from them and how they are similar:

Poem	Content	Language	Structure
'I Like to See It Lap the Miles'	This poem is about . . .	Written as an extended metaphor as Dickinson compares . . .	Written in stanzas, each verse four lines. No rhy . . . or rhy . . . but Dickinson suggests movement by using enjambement. The verses and lines flow on just like . . .
'Night Mail'	is about . . .	Uses repetition	Stanzas vary because . . .
'From a Railway Carriage'			

Write an essay exploring the similarities and differences of the three poems.

I Like to See It Lap the Miles

I like to see it lap the miles
And lick the valleys up,
And stop to feed itself at tanks
And then prodigious step

Around a pile of mountains,　　5
And supercilious peer
In shanties by the sides of roads,
And then a quarry pare

To fit its sides, and crawl between,
Complaining all the while　　10
In horrid, hooting stanza,
Then chase itself down hill

And neigh like Boanerges,
Then prompter than a star,
Stop, docile and omnipotent,　　15
At its own stable door.

Emily Dickinson

1 Presenting Journeys (groups of four)

Prepare a dramatic presentation of one of these poems. You may want to:

- add sound effects to emphasise the rhythm of the railway carriage
- show how Stevenson creates the sound and rhythm of a train
- show how Auden changes the rhythm in 'Night Mail' – explain why he does this.

2 Advertising

The railways have decided to base an advertising campaign on these two poems. Choose *one* of the following:

- Create designs for a poster campaign using the content of the poems as inspiration.
- Create a television advertisement – make a storyboard first, and include lines from the poems in the final presentation.

3 Looking Back, or A Modern Alternative

These poems were written in different centuries.

(a) Which do you think is the nineteenth-century poem and which was written in the twentieth century? Make sure you find lines from each poem to support your opinion.

(b) Make a list of things you might see that are not mentioned in the poems. Use this list and develop the spider diagram below to draft your own railway poem. Try to use rhythm like Stevenson and Auden to create and mirror the feeling of movement.

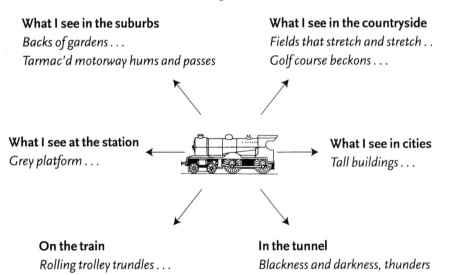

What I see in the suburbs
Backs of gardens . . .
Tarmac'd motorway hums and passes

What I see in the countryside
Fields that stretch and stretch . .
Golf course beckons . . .

What I see at the station
Grey platform . . .

What I see in cities
Tall buildings . . .

On the train
Rolling trolley trundles . . .
Nodding faces . . .

In the tunnel
*Blackness and darkness, thunders
    and rumbles*

Night Mail

This is the night mail crossing the border,
Bringing the cheque and the postal order,
Letters for the rich, letters for the poor,
The shop at the corner and the girl next door.
Pulling up Beattock, a steady climb –   5
The gradient's against her, but she's on time.

Past cotton grass and moorland boulder
Shovelling white steam over her shoulder,
Snorting noisily as she passes
Silent miles of wind-bent grasses.   10

Birds turn their heads as she approaches,
Stare from the bushes at her black-faced coaches.
Sheep-dogs cannot turn her course,
They slumber on with paws across.
In the farm she passes no one wakes,   15
But a jug in the bedroom gently shakes.

Dawn freshens, the climb is done.
Down towards Glasgow she descends
Towards the steam tugs yelping down the glade of
     cranes,
Towards the fields of apparatus, the furnaces   20
Set on the dark plain like gigantic chessmen.
All Scotland waits for her:
In the dark glens, beside the pale-green lochs
Men long for news.

Letters of thanks, letters from banks,   25
Letters of joy from girl and boy,
Receipted bills and invitations
To inspect new stock or visit relations,
And applications for situations
And timid lovers' declarations   30
And gossip, gossip from all the nations,
News circumstantial, news financial,
Letters with holiday snaps to enlarge in,
Letters with faces scrawled in the margin
Letters from uncles, cousins, and aunts,   35
Letters to Scotland from the South of France,
Letters of condolence to Highlands and
     Lowlands,
Notes from overseas to Hebrides –

Written on paper of every hue,
The pink, the violet, the white and the blue,   40
The chatty, the catty, the boring, adoring,
The cold and official and the heart outpouring,
Clever, stupid, short and long,
The typed and printed and the spelt all wrong.

Thousands are still asleep   45
Dreaming of terrifying monsters,
Or of friendly tea beside the band at Cranston's
     or Crawford's,

Asleep in working Glasgow, asleep in well-set
     Edinburgh,
Asleep in granite Aberdeen,
They continue their dreams;   50
And shall wake soon and long for letters,
And none will hear the postman's knock
Without a quickening of the heart,
For who can hear and feel himself forgotten?

                              W. H. Auden

From a Railway Carriage

Faster than fairies, faster than witches,
Bridges and houses, hedges and ditches;
And charging along like troops in a battle,
All through the meadows the horses and cattle:
All of the sights of the hill and the plain   5
Fly as thick as driving rain;
And ever again, in the wink of an eye,
Painted stations whistle by.

Here is a child who clambers and scrambles,
All by himself and gathering brambles;   10
Here is a tramp who stands and gazes;
And there is the green for stringing the daisies!
Here is a cart run away in the road
Lumping along with man and load;
And here is a mill, and there is a river: 15
Each a glimpse and gone for ever!

                    Robert Louis Stevenson

PEOPLE AND RELATIONSHIPS

1 A Middle English Puzzle (pairs)

This poem was written over five hundred years ago, when the English language was a little different but parents were still giving the same advice! With a bit of imagination and patience you should be able to work out what Chaucer is saying (particularly if you use the clue in the title).

Read the poem through quickly – don't worry about difficult words. One of you play the father, the other his son. Use your imagination, bits of the poem, and modern English to present a one-minute edited version of the father's advice to his son.

2 Middle English Explained (groups of four)

Chaucer's language is called *Middle English*. Here are some of the words which have changed over the last five hundred years:

Line 3	'bless'	protect by making the sign of the cross
Line 5	'eke'	also
Line 6	'avise'	consider, think carefully about
Line 8	'spilt'	spoilt, ruined
Line 8	'clerkes'	clergymen, scholars
Line 9	'avisely'	prudently, carefully
Line 10	'shent'	harmed
Line 12	'but'	except
Line 14	'lere'	learn
Line 17	'muckle'	much
Line 17	'evil avised'	ill considered, not thought through
Line 21	'wost'	consider, think about
Line 21	'rakel'	rash, hasty
Line 24	'a-two'	in two

3 A Middle English Dictionary

Write a brief Middle English dictionary which explains all the words in the poem that a modern reader might not understand. Organise this in alphabetical order, add other words, explain whether the word is a noun or verb, and extend the explanations.

Controlling the Tongue

My son, keep well thy tongue, and keep thy friend.
A wicked tongue is worse than a fiend;
My son, from a fiend men may them bless.
My son, God of his endless goodness
Walled a tongue with teeth and lips eke,   5
For man should him avise what he speak.
My son, full oft, for too much speech
Hath many a man been spilt, as clerkès teach;
But for little speech avisely
Is no man shent, to speak generally.   10
My son, thy tongue shouldst thou restrain
At all time, but when thou dost thy pain
To speak of God, in honour and prayer.
The first virtue, son, if thou wilt lere,
Is to restrain and keep well thy tongue;   15
Thus learn children when that they been young.
My son, of muckle speaking evil-avised,
Where less speaking had enough sufficed,
Cometh muckle harm; thus was me told and taught.
In muckle speech sin wanteth nought.   20
Wost thou whereof a rakel tongue serveth?
Right as a sword forcutteth and forcarveth
An arm a-two, my dear son, right so
A tongue cutteth friendship all a-two.

Geoffrey Chaucer

1 **Three Bits of Advice (groups of three)**

Choose three pieces of advice given in the poem, and

> *either*
> - present the advice in the form of a cartoon
>   *or*
> - imagine that 'the little children' referred to in the poem did not take much notice of the advice given. Improvise the scene after they have left, as the hosts complain about guests who spit or throw bones onto the floor!

2 **Rhyming Couplets (pairs)**

Much of this poem is written in rhyming pairs of lines, or *couplets*.

Find one couplet of advice and prepare a reading of it using both voices. You will need to think about what tone of voice to use: kindly, authoritative, sharp?

Present your reading and explain the tone you chose.

3 **Behaviour When Away From Home (pairs)**

This anonymous poet gives advice on table manners. You might wish to advise on other matters. Draw a diagram like this to brainstorm what advice you will give and to whom.

Use it as a plan for writing your own poem:

To: Parents
On: How to behave at parents' evening:

> 1 *Don't wear that embarrassing jacket / skirt / tie.*
> 2 *Don't mention what I said about . . .*

To: Your friend
On: What is a true friend?

ADVICE

To:
On:

To:
On:

Manners at Table When Away from Home

Little children, here ye may lere,
Much courtesy that is written here.

Look thine hands be washen clean,
That no filth in thy nails be seen.
Take thou no meat till grace be said   5
And till thou see all things arrayed.
Look, my son, that thou not sit
Till the ruler of the house thee bid.
And at thy meat, in the beginning,
Look on poor men that thou think: 10
For the full stomach ever fails
To understand what the hungry ails.
Eat not thy meat too hastily,
Abide and eat easily.
Carve not thy bread too thin,   15
Nor break it not in twain:
The morsels that thou beginnest to touch
Cast them not in thy pouch.
Put not thy fingers in thy dish,
Neither in flesh, neither in fish;   20
Put not thy meat into the salt
(Into thy cellar that thy salt halt)
But lay it fair on thy trencher
Before thee, that is honour.

Pick not thine ears nor thy nostrils,   25
If thou do, men will say thou com'st of churls.
And while thy meat in thy mouth is
Drink thou not – forget not this.
Eat thy meat by small morsels,
Fill not thy mouth as doeth rascals.   30
Pick not thy teeth with thy knife;
In no company begin thou strife.

CONTINUED ☞

4 Glossary (groups of four)

A glossary is used to explain difficult words like the following:

Line 1	'lere'	learn
Line 22	'halt'	holds
Line 23	'trencher'	plate
Line 26	'churls'	peasants, menials
Line 33	'pottage'	soup, stew
Line 36	'able'	seemly, polite
Line 39	'bulk'	belch
Line 40	'cot'	a poor, humble cottage
Line 47	'rede'	advise

Choose a section of the poem you find difficult and present it to the class using a combination of the original verse, explanation and drama.

5 Christian children all must be / Mild, obedient, good as He

The Victorians lived 400 years later than the poet advising on 'correct' behaviour at table. Books, hymns and carols (see the lines above) were written advising children about good morals, and pictures put on walls warning of what would happen if they misbehaved. Belloc's poem 'Matilda' (page 87) is one grimly humorous example. Here's another:

Shock-headed Peter

Shock-headed Peter! There he stands,
With his horrid hair and hands.
See, his nails are never cut;
They are grim'd as black as soot;
And, the sloven, I declare,
He has never comb'd his hair;
Anything to me is sweeter
Than to see Shock-headed Peter.

Respond to these sources by:
  (a) Writing a children's rights charter saying what you think teenagers should be allowed to do.
  (b) Listing what you learn about life in 1480 and in Victorian times.

Manners at Table When Away from Home (continued)

And when thou hast thy pottage done,
Out of thy dish put thou thy spoon.
Nor spit thou not over the table   35
Nor thereupon – for it is not able.
Lay not thine elbow nor thy fist
Upon the table whilst thou eat'st.
Bulk not, as a bean were in thy throat,
As a churl that comes out of a cot.   40
And if thy meat be of great price
Be ware of it, or thou art not wise.

Bite not thy meat, but carve it clean:
Be well ware no drop be seen.
When thou eatest gape not too wide,   45
That thy mouth be seen on every side.
And son, be ware, I rede, of one thing,
Blow neither in thy meat nor in thy drink.

And cast not thy bones unto the floor,
But lay them fair on thy trencher.   50
Keep clean thy cloth before all
And sit thou still, whatso befall,
Till grace be said unto the end,
And till thou have washen with thy friend.
And spit not in thy basin,   55
My sweet son, that thou washest in;
And arise up soft and still,
And jangle neither with Jack nor Jill,
But take thy leave of thy host lowly,
And thank him with thine heart highly.   60
Then men will say thereafter
That 'A gentleman was here.'

Anon

1 Here Lies (pairs)

Imagine this is the tombstone of a poor poet who loved a woman from a noble and wealthy family. He could not tell her of his love and eventually died of a broken heart. On his tombstone is a line from one of his poems.

Love is love, in Beggars, as in Kings.

Use this clue to prepare a roleplay in which the poet finally manages to speak to the lady he loves.

2 Deep and Passionate Feelings (pairs)

Read Dyer's poem aloud in pairs. Many of the metaphors compare his deep, intense love to other things like deep water, or sparks.

Prepare a picture chart which explains three of Dyer's metaphors. For an example, see page 14.

3 'Still Waters Run Deep' (pairs)

(a) This *aphorism* (wise saying) has been passed down through the centuries. Copy, then illustrate and explain it.

(b) Read lines 7–12 of the poem. Which of these lines is like the aphorism? What other aphorisms do you know? Can you explain them?

> *Don't cry over . . .*
> *Less haste more . . .*

4 The Love Letter Never Sent

After his death a letter was found written by the poet to the lady he loved. Write your version of his letter. This glossary might help:

'gall'	impudence or cheek
'splene'	ill-temper, anger
'haires'	could be the slim and swift hare, or hairs
'sourse'	source, or start
'diall'	clock face
'hart'	heart

5 Spelling Test (pairs)

Words were spelt differently in the sixteenth century. Write down every word in the poem that has a different spelling from today's. Then write an explanation of how you think the spelling of words has changed.

The Lowest Trees Have Tops

The lowest Trees have tops, the Ante her gall,
The flie her splene, the little sparkes their heate:
The slender haires cast shadowes, though but small,
And Bees have stings, although they be not great:
   Seas have their sourse, & so have shallow springs,
   And love is love, in Beggars, as in Kings.

Where rivers smoothest run, deepe are the foords,
The Diall stirres, yet none perceives it moove:
The firmest faith is in the fewest wordes,
The Turtles cannot sing, and yet they love:
   True Harts have eyes, & eares, no tongs to speake,
   They heare, & see, and sigh, and then they breake.

Sir Edward Dyer

1 Age Equals Wrinkles, Youth Equals Pleasure (pairs)

Think about the differences between someone who is in school and an elderly person. You might want to consider appearance, personality, beliefs, movement, temperament and interests.

Copy this table. Carry on and write down many more 'opposites' between age and youth.

Age	Youth
slow and hesitant	*swift and bold*
shuffles and . . .	*runs and . . .*
cares and concerns	*hot tempered*

Now read the two poems. Add Shakespeare's thoughts about youth and age and Yeats's reflections on old age to your table.

2 Switch (pairs)

Shakespeare often uses the final lines of his sonnets to change the poem's meaning. Read the last four lines of 'Age and Youth' carefully. Is Shakespeare saying he hates age and longs for youth, or does he adore one young person in particular? Who is this 'Shepheard'?

- Talk about the final lines of 'Age and Youth'. Write an explanation for the class.
- Is there a switch in meaning between Yeats's title (which suggests the old men 'admire themselves') and the meaning of the rest of the poem?

3 Poetry or Prose

Use the table above to write *one* of the following:

- A poem called 'Age and Youth'. As this is poetry, keep the lines short. Try to use the same repetition of the words 'youth' and 'age' as Shakespeare does in lines 2–8. This will give your poem form and structure.
- A poem about an old man or woman which uses inserts of speech like Yeats's.
- A piece of prose called 'Age and Youth' with one paragraph describing an old man, the next his grandson. You could develop this by delving into what each thinks. Or you could tell a story of a conflict which arises between an older person and a youth at work, at school or at home.

Age and Youth

Crabbed age and youth cannot live together,
Youth is full of pleasance, Age is full of care,
Youth like summer morne, Age like winter weather,
Youth like summer brave, Age like winter bare.
Youth is full of sport, Age's breath is short,
Youth is nimble, Age is lame,
Youth is hot and bold, Age is weake and cold,
Youth is wild, and Age is tame.
    Age I doe abhor thee, Youth I doe adore thee,
        O my love, my love is young:
    Age I doe defie thee. Oh sweet Shepheard hie thee:
        For methinks thou stay'st too long.

William Shakespeare

The Old Men Admiring Themselves in the Water

I heard the old, old men say,
'Everything alters,
And one by one we drop away.'
They had hands like claws, and their knees
Were twisted like the old thorn-trees
By the waters.
I heard the old, old men say,
'All that's beautiful drifts away
Like the waters.'

W. B. Yeats

1 The Perfect Woman?

Describe what the perfect man or woman might be like. Do you think he or she exists?

2 Shakespeare's Perfect Woman (pairs)

Read the poem opposite.

(a) Choose a section you like and perform the lines using a mixture of Shakespeare's language, modern English, *tableaux* and mime.

(b) Compare the woman that Shakespeare describes with your first ideas of the perfect woman. Present your conclusions to the class. You may want to draw a labelled sketch of Shakespeare's mistress, using your own explanation and words from the poem. Or you might present your findings in a table like this:

Shakespeare's mistress	The perfect woman or person
Eyes: 'nothing like the sun' suggests they are dark.	*Eyes:* dazzling blue, bright and vibrant
Lips:	

3 Ironic Language (pairs)

Irony is deliberately saying the opposite of what you mean. For example, Shakespeare opens the poem by saying that his mistress's eyes 'are nothing like the sun'. Does this mean that they are dull and lifeless or that they are dark and mysterious? What is the effect of Shakespeare's irony? Choose another image from the poem and explain how the irony works.

Sonnet 130

My mistress' eyes are nothing like the sun;
Coral is far more red than her lips' red:
If snow be white, why then her breasts are dun;
If hairs be wires, black wires grow on her head.
I have seen roses damask'd, red and white,
But no such roses see I in her cheeks;
And in some perfumes there is more delight
Than in the breath that from my mistress reeks.
I love to hear her speak, – yet well I know
That music hath a far more pleasing sound:
I grant I never saw a goddess go, –
My mistress, when she walks, treads on the ground.
   And yet, by heaven, I think my love as rare
   As any she belied with false compare.

William Shakespeare

1 Black Bile, Bad Mood (pairs)

It was believed that when you were in a melancholy (gloomy, depressed) mood, you were infected with dark, angry bile. The man in this poem is certainly in a bad mood.

One of you is the moody man, the other his wife. Prepare a presentation in which the man marches in, flings down his sword and hat and orders his wife around. Every so often freeze the action and let the wife say what she thinks of his behaviour. Use lines from the poem, and modern English, in your presentation.

Watch other pairs' presentations, take notes, then write the wife's diary entry for that night describing her husband's actions and what she thinks of him.

2 Which Conceit? (pairs)

'Conceit' has three possible meanings:

- vanity or pride
- a fanciful or imaginative idea
- a long and unusual metaphor or comparison, usually used by writers.

Which meaning of 'conceit' do you think Samuel Rowlands uses in the title of his poem? Talk about this, take notes, then present your answer to the class.

3 The State of Your Room!

Imagine the state of this man's room just before his wife and the maid leave: the hat thrown aside, the maid carrying Pearl the parrot out, the clock ('jack') muffled . . . Draw the room and label your drawing with phrases from the poem.

4 A Puzzle (pairs)

Some lines in poetry can be interpreted in different ways. As long as you can prove your interpretation using quotations from the poem you are right.

What do you think lines 7–8 mean? The following might help:
an 'almanac' is a calendar containing astrology and prediction.

Melancholy Conceit

Rapier, lie there! and there, my hat and feather!
    Draw my silk curtain to obscure the light,
Goose-quill and I must join awhile together:
    Lady, forbear, I pray, keep out of sight!
Call Pearl away, let one remove him hence!
Your shrieking parrot will distract my sense.

Would I were near the rogue that crieth, 'Black!'
    'Buy a new almanac!' doth vex me too:
Forbid the maid she wind not up the jack!
    Take hence my watch, it makes too much ado!
Let none come at me, dearest friend or kin:
    Whoe'er it be I am not now within.

Samuel Rowlands

1 Metaphors (pairs)

William Drummond uses metaphors or word pictures to compare the death of his love to a gloomy night robbed of its light. This comparison extends over the opening eight lines. Read them aloud, changing reader at each punctuation mark.

Create a metaphor word and picture chart for display. Draw, label and explain Drummond's metaphors. An example is given here.

A beautiful star shines with rays like strands of golden hair. A spiteful and vicious cloud hides this beauty from view.

2 Rhetorical Questions (pairs)

Read the questions in the second part of the poem and discuss why the poet has used this form of question which doesn't expect an answer.

One of you read aloud the powerful rhetorical questions of the final lines. Your partner responds with replies that you think Drummond might have given.

3 Meanings and Spellings (pairs)

This poem was written over four hundred years ago, when language and spelling were different.

Write an explanation of lines 9–14 using this glossary and the picture opposite to help:

'vaunt'	boast
'raine'	reign, or rule over
'plaine'	complain, speak mournfully

As in a Duskie and Tempestuous Night

As in a duskie and tempestuous Night,
A Starre is wont to spreade her Lockes of Gold,
And while her pleasant Rayes abroad are roll'd,
Some spitefull Cloude doth robbe us of her Sight:
(Faire Soule) in this black Age so shin'd thou bright, 5
And made all Eyes with Wonder thee beholde,
Till uglie *Death* depriving us of Light,
In his grimme mistie Armes thee did enfolde.
Who more shall vaunt true Beautie heere to see?
What Hope doth more in any Heart remaine, 10
That such Perfections shall his *Reason* raine?
If Beautie with thee borne too died with thee?
   World, plaine no more of *Love*, nor count his Harmes,
   With his pale Trophees *Death* hath hung his Armes.

William Drummond of Hawthornden

1 Editing the poem (pairs)

'My Cat Jeoffry' is a long poem which can be read and interpreted in different ways. Read the whole of the poem on pages 61, 63 and 65, and think about which interpretation you want to try.

In your pairs reduce the poem to a twenty-line interpretation. Before you begin, agree which aspect of the poem you will focus on.

Interpretation A emphasises the cat's movements.

My Cat Jeoffry – the movement version

Rolls, kicks,
Sharpens his paws by wood . . .

Interpretation B emphasises the religious expression of the poem. Notice how the repetition of 'For' sounds biblical. Include Smart's use of Jeoffry as a symbol of goodness and light, fighting against God's 'adversary' (enemy), the Devil.

My Cat Jeoffry – the religious version

For he is the servant of the Living God,
For he worships in his way
For he leaps, blessing God.
For he keeps . . .

Interpretation C emphasises the speaker's delight in Jeoffry – his use of 'my' cat. Focus on the positive descriptions of the cat, his beauty and the positive language: 'he is', 'he counteracts', 'he keeps'.

My Cat Jeoffry – the admiration version

My cat Jeoffry
Is the servant of the Living God
For having considered God he will consider his neighbour . . .

Read your edited version of the poem to the class. Create a display of edited poems, illustrations and explanations.

My Cat Jeoffry

For I will consider my cat Jeoffry.
For he is the servant of the Living God, duly and daily serving Him.
For at the first glance of the Glory of God in the East he worships
    in his way.
For is this done by wreathing his body seven times round with elegant
    quickness.
For then he leaps up to catch the musk, which is the blessing of God
    on his prayer.   5
For he rolls upon prank to work it in.
For having done duty, and received blessing, he begins to consider
    himself.
For this he performs in ten degrees.
For first he looks upon his forepaws to see if they are clean.
For secondly he kicks up behind to clear away there.   10
For thirdly he works it upon stretch with the forepaws extended.
For fourthly he sharpens his paws by wood.
For fifthly he washes himself.
For sixthly he rolls upon wash.
For seventhly he fleas himself, that he may not be interrupted upon
    the beat.   15

CONTINUED☞

2 Alliteration in the Poem (pairs)

Alliteration is where two words near each other are linked together by starting with the same letter:

For at the first glance of the Glory of God in the East he worships in his way

The alliterative words have been circled. This table shows how the alliterative words emphasise the sense of the line.

Line using alliteration	Alliterative words	Picture created	Effect of alliteration
'For at the first glance of the Glory of God'	glance Glory God		1 The alliteration links the cat to the object it is looking at. Action → Object 'glances' → sun

Find examples of alliteration in the opening of the poem and add them to your table.

3 Looking at the Tone of the Poem

Smart spent several years in a lunatic asylum, although today we wouldn't consider his condition to be a form of madness. His moods varied greatly and this is reflected in his writing. Do you think 'My Cat Jeoffry' is sad or optimistic? Use the table below to structure your ideas.

Mr Depressed	Mr Optimistic
'Poor Jeoffry! Poor Jeoffry! the rat has bit thy throat.' Unhappy event as the rat jumps and bites . . .	'For when he takes his prey he plays with it to give it a chance.' Shows the cat as playful rather than a killer

My Cat Jeoffry (continued)

For eighthly he rubs himself a-gainst a post.
For ninthly he looks up for his instructions.
For tenthly he goes in quest of food.
For having considered God and himself he will consider his neighbour.
For if he meets another cat he will kiss her in kindness. 20
For when he takes his prey he plays with it to give it a chance.
For one mouse in seven escapes by his dallying.
For when his day's work is done his business more properly begins.
For he keeps the Lord's watch in the night against the Adversary.
For he counteracts the powers of darkness by his electrical skin
    and glaring eyes. 25
For he counteracts the Devil, who is death, by brisking about the life.
For in his morning orisons he loves the sun and the sun loves him.
For he is of the tribe of Tiger.
For the Cherub Cat is a term of the Angel Tiger.
For he has the subtlety and hiss of the serpent, which in goodness
    he suppresses. 30
For he will not do destruction, if he is well-fed, neither will he spit
    without provocation.
For he purrs in thankfulness, when God tells him he's a good Cat.
For he is an instrument for the children to learn benevolence upon.
For every house is incomplete without him and a blessing is lacking
    in the spirit.
For the Lord commanded Moses concerning the cats at the
    departure of the Children of Israel from Egypt. 35
For every family had one cat at least in the bag.
For the English cats are the best in Europe.
For he is the cleanest in the use of his forepaws of any quadrupede.
For the dexterity of his defence is an instance of the love of God
    to him exceedingly.
For he is the quickest to his mark of any creature. 40
For he is tenacious of his point.
For he is a mixture of gravity and waggery.
For he knows that God is his Saviour.
For there is nothing sweeter than his peace when at rest.
For there is nothing brisker than his life when in motion. 45

CONTINUED ☞

4 Collecting Evidence (pairs)

Before writing about the poem you will need to read and discuss it all in detail. Keep a note of your ideas and the phrases to which they refer. Order your notes in the following way:

(a) The story:	What we learn about Jeoffry
	What Jeoffry means to the speaker
(b) The style:	The language Smart uses
	Any particularly descriptive lines
(c) Your opinion:	Does the poem describe the cat well?
	Is it a sad or happy poem?
	Did you enjoy it?

5 Drafting a Literary Critical Essay (individual)

Use your notes to answer this essay question: 'Discuss the content and style of Christopher Smart's "My Cat Jeoffry"'. The structure below may help you.

INTRODUCTION

Three to four sentences explaining what the poem is about and the style it is written in. The first sentence should name the poet and poem, for example:

Christopher Smart's poem 'My Cat Jeoffry' is about . . .

PARAGRAPH 1

Discuss the content but do not retell the story. Explain how the story is structured (whether it begins at the beginning) and what kind of a story it is (whether it is about key events or lots of little incidents, whether it is optimistic or negative).

PARAGRAPH 2

Discuss the style of the poem. In writing this paragraph refer to:

The structure: Smart's use of repetition at the beginning of lines.

Diction: the poet's choice of language, his descriptive phrases.

Tone: whether it is a happy or depressed poem.

CONCLUSION

Summarise your argument in two or three sentences. Do the content and style work well together?

My Cat Jeoffry (continued)

For he is of the Lord's poor and so indeed is he called by benevolence
    perpetually – Poor Jeoffry! poor Jeoffry! the rat has bit thy throat.
For I bless the name of the Lord Jesus that Jeoffry is better.
For the divine spirit comes about his body to sustain it in complete cat.
For his tongue is exceeding pure so that it has in purity what it wants
    in music.
For he is docile and can learn certain things.   50
For he can set up with gravity which is patience upon approbation.
For he can fetch and carry, which is patience in employment.
For he can jump over a stick which is patience upon proof positive.
For he can spraggle upon waggle at the word of command.
For he can jump from an eminence into his master's bosom.   55
For he can catch the cork and toss it again.
For he is hated by the hypocrite and miser.
For the former is afraid of detection.
And the latter refuses the charge.
For he camels his back to bear the first notion of business.   60
For he is good to think on, if a man would express himself neatly.
For he made a great figure in Egypt for his signal services.
For he killed the Ichneumon-rat very pernicious by land.
For his ears are so acute that they sting again.
For from this proceeds the passing quickness of his attention.   65
For by stroking of him I have found out electricity.
For I perceive God's light about him both wax and fire.
For the electrical fire is the spiritual substance, which God sends from
    heaven to sustain the bodies of both man and beast.
For God has blessed him in the variety of his movements.
For, tho he cannot fly, he is an excellent clamberer.   70
For his motions upon the face of the earth are more than any other
    quadrupede.
For he can tread to all the measures upon the music.
For he can swim for life.
For he can creep.

Christopher Smart

1 Tell Beau Off (groups of six)

This poem is spoken by a dog-owner telling his spaniel off for catching and killing a young bird.

Prepare a reading of the poem using all voices in the group. You might decide to add actions and to emphasise the master's anger with his dog.

2 Reasons for the Owner's Anger (pairs)

Note down the many reasons Beau's owner gives for his disappointment and anger with his dog.

Use these to make a display poster that might go above Beau's kennel telling of what a dog should and should not do. You might use some well-chosen lines from the poem as slogans.

3 What Might Beau Respond? (pairs)

We hear a lot from the owner, but nothing from Beau. What might be the dog's response?

Read the owner's complaints and note down any excuses the dog might make for his behaviour. For example:

Instinct took over from training.

Use your list to write a short poem called 'Beau's Reply'. Assume he is at least as intelligent as his owner and, if you can, use the same rhythm and rhyme scheme:

A Spaniel, Beau, that fares like you,	(a)
Well-fed, and at his ease,	(b)
Should wiser be, than to pursue	(a)
Each trifle that he sees.	(b)

If you look at page 69 you will see that William Cowper also gave Beau a voice.

On a Spaniel Called Beau Killing a Young Bird

A Spaniel, Beau, that fares like you,
    Well-fed, and at his ease,
Should wiser be, than to pursue
    Each trifle that he sees.

But you have kill'd a tiny bird,   5
    Which flew not till to-day,
Against my orders, whom you heard
    Forbidding you the prey.

Nor did you kill, that you might eat,
    And ease a doggish pain,   10
For him, though chas'd with furious heat,
    You left where he was slain.

Nor was he of the thievish sort,
    Or one whom blood allures.
But innocent was all his sport,   15
    Whom you have torn for yours.

My dog! what remedy remains,
    Since, teach you all I can,
I see you, after all my pains,
    So much resemble man!   20

William Cowper

1 Comparing the Two (pairs)

Read 'Beau's Reply'. Do you agree with the owner or the dog? Note the main points of the two sides of the argument in columns like this:

Owner's point of view
Dog, well fed and looked after,
should know better,

Beau's point of view
Instinct counts for more
than logic or owner's voice.

Use these notes to explain whose point of view you agree with and why.

Does the way Cowper writes have anything to do with your opinion? Look closely at the tone of Beau's last verse.

When a writer adds a double edge or meaning to the verse, this is called *irony*. Cowper's two poems could be an ironical comment on what society finds unnatural. Explain the two things presented as 'unnatural'. Here is a clue:

- *Killing . . .*
- *Writing . . .*

Write a few sentences on why this is ironical.

2 Hunting (groups of four)

In Cowper's time dogs were used for hunting animals like deer, foxes and badgers. Many forms of hunting are now illegal, although some are still practised.

Divide into two pairs to debate whether or not hunting should be illegal. Your personal opinion is not important in the debate. Cowper shows how we should consider two points of view.

Pair A: Argue that all forms of hunting should be illegal.
Pair B: Argue that we should have the right to make up our own minds about hunting without needing laws.

Begin by making notes to support your case:

Pair A
Hunting of badgers is cruel . . .

Pair B
The fox is a pest . . .

You should undertake some research to argue your case well. Once you have done this, debate the issue.

Use your notes and the debate as source material for a discursive essay: 'All forms of hunting should be illegal. Discuss.'

Beau's Reply

Sir! when I flew to seize the bird,
    In spite of your command,
A louder voice than yours I heard
    And harder to withstand:

You cried – Forbear! – but in my breast   5
    A mightier cried – Proceed!
'Twas nature, Sir, whose strong behest
    Impell'd me to the deed.

Yet much as nature I respect,
    I ventur'd once to break   10
(As you perhaps may recollect)
    Her precept, for your sake;

And when your linnet, on a day,
    Passing his prison-door,
Had flutter'd all his strength away,   15
    And panting press'd the floor,

Well knowing him a sacred thing,
    Not destin'd to my tooth,
I only kiss'd his ruffled wing,
    And lick'd the feathers smooth.   20

Let my obedience then excuse
    My disobedience now,
Nor some reproof yourself refuse
    From your aggriev'd Bow-wow!

If killing birds be such a crime,   25
    (which I can hardly see)
What think you, Sir, of killing Time
    With verse address'd to me?

William Cowper

1 **Epitaph for Lucy (pairs)**

Wordsworth's poem expresses intense sadness for the death of Lucy. Read it aloud using different tones and varying the pace where appropriate.

(a) Use the information in the poem to write an *epitaph* for Lucy – a short statement about her that could be carved on her tombstone. You might like to include some of Wordsworth's words.

(b) The title of the second poem, 'The Despairing Lover', suggests that this too might be a sad poem about an unhappy lover. Read it and decide on a tone and pace to present it. Is it sad?

Write a paragraph contrasting the content, style and tone of 'The Despairing Lover' and 'Lucy'.

2 **Metaphors (pairs)**

A *metaphor* describes one thing in terms of another. For example, in verse 2 Wordsworth refers to Lucy as a beautiful violet: 'A violet by a mossy stone / Half hidden from the eye!'

Where is the violet, and why is it like Lucy?

Choose two other metaphors and explain them in words and pictures.

Lucy

She dwelt among the untrodden ways
    Beside the springs of Dove,
A Maid whom there were none to praise
    And very few to love:

A violet by a mossy stone
    Half hidden from the eye!
– Fair as a star, when only one
    Is shining in the sky.

She lived unknown, and few could know
    When Lucy ceased to be;
But she is in her grave, and, oh,
    The difference to me!

William Wordsworth

The Despairing Lover

Distracted with care
For Phyllis the fair,
Since nothing could move her,
Poor Damon, her lover,
Resolves in despair   5
No longer to languish,
Nor bear so much anguish:
But, mad with his love,
To a precipice goes,
Where a leap from above   10
Would soon finish his woes.

When in rage he came there,
Beholding how steep
The sides did appear,
And the bottom how deep;   15
His torments projecting,
And sadly reflecting,
That a lover forsaken
A new love may get,
But a neck, when once broken,   20
Can never be set:
And, that he could die
Whenever he would,
But, that he could live
But as long as he could: 25
How grievous soever
The torment might grow,
He scorn'd to endeavour
To finish it so.
But bold, unconcern'd   30
At thoughts of the pain,
He calmly return'd
To his cottage again.

William Walsh

1 Reject Him (groups of three)

The poem tells the story of a widower (a man whose wife has died) called Roger. He sets out to win the favours of Nell, the young milk-maid. The poem can be read by three voices:

THE NARRATOR   tells the story.
ROGER   speaks first and asks to carry Nell's pail.
NELL   gives Roger several blunt replies.

Prepare a performance reading of the poem. You might want to include actions.

2 The Gossips

Write details about the characters and events on a table like this:

Roger	Nell	What happens
Been sad (doleful) for four months since his wife died...	Independent: won't let Roger carry her bucket...	Roger walks across the green determined to meet Nell. He is smiling.

Imagine that a group of villagers watch Roger go smiling to meet Nell on the green. Use the ideas on your table to create a drama in which these village gossips discuss this latest incident.

3 Using Language

Elizabeth Hands uses different techniques to express meaning. The diagram below explains two of them. Copy and finish it.

Monosyllable – a word of one short beat	Irony –saying the opposite of what you mean to make fun of someone or something
Many of Nell's words are short (monosyllabic). An example is . . . The poet does this because . . .	The poet decribes Roger as 'doleful', unhappy for a _____ eighteen weeks. By line 4 he is _____, suggesting that he has not been sad for long . . .

Talk about whether these techniques make you prefer a particular character.

The Widower's Courtship

Roger a doleful widower,
   Full eighteen weeks had been,
When he, to meet the milk-maid Nell
   Came smiling o'er the green.

Blithe as a lad of seventeen,   5
   He thus accosted Nell;
Give me your pail, I'll carry it
   For you, if you think well.

Says Nell, Indeed my milking-pail
   You shall not touch, I vow;   10
I've carried it myself before,
   And I can carry it now.

So side by side they walked awhile,
   Then he at last did say;
My inclination is to come   15
   And see you, if I may.

Nell understood his meaning well,
   And briskly answered she;
You may see me any time,
   If you look where I be.   20

Says he, but hear me yet awhile,
   I've something more to tell;
I gladly would a sweetheart be
   Unto you, Mistress Nell.

A sweetheart I don't want, says Nell,   25
   Kind Sir, and if you do,
Another you may seek, for I
   Am not the lass for you.

When she had bade him this reply,
   He'd nothing more to say   30
But – Nelly good night to you,
   And homeward went his way.

Elizabeth Hands

1 Alternatives (groups of four)

It is said that we live in a consumer society where people are defined by what they can afford to buy. Could you give up consumer luxuries? List ten current consumer items. Next to each write a natural alternative.

2 Old Meg's Alternative

A student commenting on Keats's poem said she likes this poem because:

Meg Merrilies seems to have an alternative to everything she does not possess. For example, she did not have a proper house so she lived out of doors and slept on brown heath turf because she did not have a bed.

(a) Continue this explanation of Meg's alternatives

(b) Use all of your 'alternative' information to construct a poem about living an alternative life-style.

3 Telling the Tale (two groups of four)

These two poems tell different tales of gypsy characters. Read them both.

GROUP A

Re-read 'The Gipsy Laddie' using different voices for each character and the narrator. Note down eight key events in the poem. Use this information to present:

- an improvisation in which the squire's servants gossip about the lady who ran away with Davy, the master's efforts to persuade her to return, and what happened to her
- a commentary on the view of 'gipsies' given in this poem. Is it a stereotype?

GROUP B

Re-read Keats's poem describing Meg Merrilies the gypsy. Jot down notes about her appearance, her way of life and her actions. Use these notes to present:

- an improvisation in which characters who admire Meg remember what she was like and what she used to do
- a commentary on the view of gypsies given in this poem.

After you have heard the presentations, talk about the different views each poet presents.

Meg Merrilies

Old Meg she was a Gipsey,
    And liv'd upon the Moors;
Her bed it was the brown heath turf,
    And her house was out of doors.

Her apples were swart blackberries,   5
    Her currants, pods o'broom;
Her wine was dew of the wild white rose,
    Her book a churchyard tomb.

Her Brothers were the craggy hills,
    Her Sisters larchen trees;   10
Alone with her great family
    She liv'd as she did please.

No breakfast had she many a morn,
    No dinner many a noon,
And, 'stead of supper, she would stare   15
    Full hard against the moon.

But every morn, of woodbine fresh
    She made her garlanding,
And, every night, the dark glen Yew
    She wove, and she would sing.   20

And with her fingers, old and brown,
    She plaited Mats o' Rushes,
And gave them to the cottagers
    She met among the Bushes.

Old Meg was brave as Margaret Queen   25
    And tall as Amazon;
An old red blanket cloak she wore,
    A chip hat had she on.
God rest her aged bones somewhere!
    She died full long agone!   30

John Keats

The Gipsy Laddie

It was late in the night when the Squire came home
Enquiring for his lady.
His servant made a sure reply:
She's gone with the gipsum Davy.
    Rattle tum a gipsum gipsum   5
    Rattle tum a gipsum Davy.

O go catch up my milk-white steed,
The black one's not so speedy,
I'll ride all night till broad daylight,
Or overtake my lady.   10

He rode and he rode till he came to the town,
He rode till he came to Barley.
The tears came rolling down his cheeks,
And then he spied his lady.

It's come go back, my dearest dear,   15
Come go back, my honey;
It's come go back, my dearest dear,
And you never shall lack for money.

I won't go back, my dearest dear,
I won't go back, my honey;   20
For I wouldn't give a kiss from gipsum's lips
For you and all your money.

It's go pull off those snow-white gloves,
A-made of Spanish leather,
And give to me your lily-white hand,   25
And bid farewell for ever.

It's she pulled off those snow-white gloves,
A-made of Spanish leather,
And gave to him her lily-white hand,
And bade farewell for ever.   30

She soon ran through her gay clothing,
Her velvet shoes and stockings;
Her gold ring off her finger's gone,
And the gold plate off her bosom.

O once I had a house and land,   35
Feather-bed and money;
But now I've come to an old straw pad
With the gipsies dancing round me.

Anon

1 Titles (pairs)

The title of a poem often gives clues about its content. Draw two spider diagrams like these and around them list what the titles make you think.

2 Sing it, Say it, Live it (groups of three)

Read the two poems aloud. Then go on and present them as mini-plays set to music.

3 Love is Weird

These poems show how strangely people behave when they are in love. Imagine you are an alien who has been sent to Earth to find out about human behaviour. Your mind is extremely logical and you have just heard the two poems performed. What will you say in your report?

4 Song

(a) Amelia Opie's 'Song' replies to a comment by Mary Ann. Write down what you think Mary Ann said. Compare your line with those of others.

(b) Work as a pair on one of these opening lines. Make it into an opening line for a song of your own. Draft the line carefully, thinking about rhythm. Then write the whole song.

Song

Yes, Mary Ann, I freely grant,
The charms of Henry's eyes I see;
But while I gaze, I something want,
I want those eyes – to gaze on me.

And I allow, in Henry's heart
   Not Envy's self a fault can see:
Yet still I must one wish impart,
   I wish that heart – to sigh for me.

Amelia Opie

I Do Not Love Thee

   I do not love thee! – no, I do not love thee!
And yet when thou art absent I am sad;
   And envy even the bright blue sky above thee,
Whose quiet stars may see thee and be glad.

   I do not love thee! – yet, I know not why,   5
Whate'er thou dost seems still well done, to me.
   And often in my solitude I sigh
That those I do love are not more like thee!

   I do not love thee! – yet, when thou art gone,
I hate the sound (though those who speak be dear)   10
   Which breaks the lingering echo of the tone
Thy voice of music leaves upon my ear.

   I do not love thee! – yet thy speaking eyes,
With their deep, bright, and most expressive blue,
   Between me and the midnight heaven arise,   15
Oftener than any eyes I ever knew.

   I know I do not love thee! yet, alas!
Others will scarcely trust my candid heart;
   And oft I catch them smiling as they pass,
Because they see me gazing where thou art.   20

Caroline Norton

1 The Secret Meeters Speak (pairs)

Read through Browning's poem and note the events that occur.

- Imagine that one of you is making the sea journey to the meeting, while the other waits for the tap at the window pane. Each of you takes it in turn to speak in role describing your travels, or your anticipation.

Frost's poem keeps you guessing about the reasons for his journey.

- Imagine one of you is the traveller through the 'dark and deep' wood, the other waits in the village as the snow falls.
  Jot down details of the journey given in the poem, adding your own imagined ideas about the reasons for the journey. Use these notes to roleplay as traveller and watcher.

2 Personification and Alliteration (pairs)

Browning writes of the excitement of meeting someone secretly at night. He emphasises this by using various poetic techniques.

Personification is when you describe something that is not human, in human terms. Read through verse 1 of the poem and note down the two lines that use personification. Explain what Browning is describing in these lines and the effect of using this technique.

Alliteration is the repetition of letters at the beginning of words. Note down examples of this and explain the effect. Where does Frost use alliteration, and why?

3 The Poet's Not There

In 'Meeting at Night', Browning avoids saying the obvious 'I was excited'. The poet's feelings are only shown through description. Similarly Frost expresses feeling by describing what he sees in a particular way: 'easy wind and downy flake'.

Write your own poem or story about an exciting event, which only uses description to express feeling. The ideas below might help you:

Use open vowel sounds
Colourful, vivid flowers bloom
Swaying cornflowers bow to the breeze

Rhyme or alliteration linking words
Elegant dragonfly wings his way
Diligent spider weaves his web

GOOD EVENT

Words should be positive
It is spring: new shoots, new life

Meeting at Night

The grey sea and the long black land;
And the yellow half-moon large and low;
And the startled little waves that leap
In fiery ringlets from their sleep,
As I gain the cove with pushing prow,
And quench its speed in the slushy sand.

Then a mile of warm sea-scented beach;
Three fields to cross till a farm appears;
A tap at the pane, the quick sharp scratch
And blue spurt of a lighted match,
And a voice less loud, through its joys and fears,
Than the two hearts beating each to each!

Robert Browning

Stopping by Woods on a Snowy Evening

Whose woods these are I think I know.
His house is in the village though;
He will not see me stopping here
To watch his woods fill up with snow.

My little horse must think it queer   5
To stop without a farmhouse near
Between the woods and frozen lake
The darkest evening of the year.

He gives his harness bells a shake
To ask if there is some mistake.   10
The only other sound's the sweep
Of easy wind and downy flake.

The woods are lovely, dark and deep.
But I have promises to keep,
And miles to go before I sleep,   15
And miles to go before I sleep.

Robert Frost

1 Jealousies (pairs)

Prepare then present the following situation.

PERSON A

You are a parent having difficulties with one of your children who is becoming increasingly jealous of the attention you give to others.

PERSON B

You are the child. You feel neglected when your parent is with other people. You have begun thinking about ways of keeping your parent's attention all to yourself.

2 Setting the Scene (groupwork)

Read the first five lines of the poem. Discuss the mood and how it is created. Referring to the following techniques may help you get started:

Creation of atmosphere through setting: the time of day, weather and location can be used to create atmosphere.

Diction: an author's choice of unusual or descriptive words can give extra information and create mood.

Personification: when an object is described using language normally reserved for humans, for example 'the happy cloud'.

3 Prediction

Having looked at the opening five lines, decide what you think the poem might be about. Make a note of your ideas to refer to later.

4 Read the Poem (groups of three)

Prepare a reading of the whole poem which highlights the action. You might decide to stop the reading at certain points in order to freeze-frame the action, or to add sound effects during the reading.

Porphyria's Lover

The rain set early in tonight,
    The sullen wind was soon awake,
It tore the elm-tops down for spite,
    And did its worst to vex the lake:
    I listened with heart fit to break.   **5**
When glided in Porphyria; straight
    She shut the cold out and the storm,
And kneeled and made the cheerless grate
    Blaze up, and all the cottage warm;
    Which done, she rose, and from her form   **10**
Withdrew the dripping cloak and shawl,
    And laid her soiled gloves by, untied
Her hat and let the damp hair fall,
    And, last, she sat down by my side
    And called me. When no voice replied,   **15**
She put my arm about her waist,
    And made her smooth white shoulder bare,
And all her yellow hair displaced,
    And, stooping, made my cheek lie there,
    And spread, o'er all, her yellow hair,   **20**
Murmuring how she loved me – she
    Too weak, for all her heart's endeavour,
To set its struggling passion free
    From pride, and vainer ties dissever,
    And give herself to me for ever.   **25**
But passion sometimes would prevail,
    Nor could tonight's gay feast restrain
A sudden thought of one so pale
    For love of her, and all in vain:
    So, she was come through wind and rain.   **30**

CONTINUED ☞

5 The Action of the Poem

Divide the poem into sections and create a series of cartoons which show the poem's action in words and pictures. Add a section to each picture which gives your feelings about events. For example:

1. The rain set in early. A man sat alone in a dark cottage.

The man seems depressed. He does nothing to help himself.

2. Porphyria comes, she lights the fire and shuts out the storm

Porphyria is a positive person who brings light and warmth.

6 Why Kill Porphyria?

Look carefully at the poem and find the two reasons Porphyria's lover gives for killing her. Discuss what this shows about his character.

7 Written Work

(a) Write a newspaper article about the murder. You may want to include interviews with family and/or neighbours.

(b) Write a police report of an interview with the murderer in which he explains what he did and why he did it. End by giving your opinions about events and recommendations about what should be done.

Porphyria's Lover (continued)

Be sure I looked up at her eyes
   Happy and proud; at last I knew
Porphyria worshipped me; surprise
   Made my heart swell, and still it grew
   While I debated what to do.   **35**
That moment she was mine, mine, fair,
   Perfectly pure and good: I found
A thing to do, and all her hair
   In one long yellow string I wound
   Three times her little throat around,   **40**
And strangled her. No pain felt she;
   I am quite sure she felt no pain.
As a shut bud that holds a bee,
   I warily oped her lids: again
   Laughed the blue eyes without a stain.   **45**
And I untightened next the tress
   About her neck; her cheek once more
Blushed bright beneath my burning kiss:
   I propped her head up as before,
   Only, this time my shoulder bore   **50**
Her head, which droops upon it still:
   The smiling rosy little head,
So glad it has its utmost will,
   That all it scorned at once is fled,
   And I, its love, am gained instead!   **55**
Porphyria's love: she guessed not how
   Her darling one wish would be heard.
And thus we sit together now,
   And all night long we have not stirred,
   And yet God has not said a word!   **60**

Robert Browning

1 What Do You Think? (groups of three)

(a) A title gives some ideas about a poem. Note down at least three things you think the poem will be about.

(b) Read the poem aloud, changing reader at each punctuation mark. Were you right in your predictions about the content of the poem? Does the title give a hint about how the poem should be read?

2 'At The Innermost Heart of a Peach' (pairs)

This shy person wishes to escape 'out of this room'. Choose three of the places the speaker would prefer to be. Copy the description of each place in the poem, then illustrate and explain what the poet's language suggests to you, for example:

'With the wasp at the innermost heart of a peach'

(I'd rather be enclosed in a tiny space with an insect that has the potential to sting than in a room with other people.)

3 Anywhere But Here (pairs)

The speaker in this poem uses imagination to transport herself out of her current situation. Write your own poem in which you imagine yourself to be anywhere but where you are.

Jot down at least ten places or situations you would rather be in. Try to use some of Greenwell's techniques: use 'with' to begin each line, and try to use a similar rhythm to the poet's.

You might want to try using a rhyme scheme in your poem. Greenwell writes in rhyming couplets, yet maintains the sense of what she is saying. Can you do this?

With things that are chainless, and tameless, and *proud*,
With the fire in the jagged thunder-*cloud*

A Scherzo: A Shy Person's Wishes

With the wasp at the innermost heart of a peach,
On a sunny wall out of tip-toe reach,
With the trout in the darkest summer pool,
With the fern-seed clinging behind its cool
Smooth frond, in the chink of an aged tree,
In the woodbine's horn with the drunken bee,
With the mouse in its nest in a furrow old,
With the chrysalis wrapped in its gauzy fold;
With things that are hidden, and safe, and bold,
With things that are timid, and shy, and free,
Wishing to be;
With the nut in its shell, with the seed in its pod,
With the corn as it sprouts in the kindly clod,
Far down where the secret of beauty shows
In the bulb of the tulip, before it blows;
With things that are rooted, and firm, and deep,
Quiet to lie, and dreamless to sleep;
With things that are chainless, and tameless, and proud
With the fire in the jagged thunder-cloud,
With the wind in its sleep, with the wind in its waking,
With the drops that go to the rainbow's making,
Wishing to be with the light leaves shaking,
Or stones in some desolate highway breaking;
Far up on the hills, where no foot surprises
The dew as it falls, or the dust as it rises;
To be couched with the beast in its torrid lair,
Or drifting on ice with the polar bear,
With the weaver at work at his quiet loom;
Anywhere, anywhere, out of this room!

Dora Greenwell

1 Interviews (pairs)

In pairs, roleplay a radio interview with Matilda's aunt after the tragic fire.

- How would Matilda's aunt feel?
- What questions would the reporter need to ask in order to get all the details from the aunt?

2 Cartoons (individual)

An editor preparing an anthology of poems for young children wants to include 'Matilda'. In order to help the children understand the poem, you have been asked to draw six cartoons to explain key moments of the story. Decide which moments you will illustrate. Draw the six pictures and add captions and quotations to each.

3 The Moral of the Story (groups of four)

(a) 'Matilda' is one of several poems written by Belloc called 'Cautionary Tales', warning children of what might happen to them if they misbehave. Write the moral lesson of 'Matilda'.

(b) Another of the tales is about a boy called Jim whose 'Friends were very good to him'. The moral of this tale is: 'Don't run away from people looking after you'.

Devise and present an improvisation which shows this moral. After showing your plays, find the original poem and see if you were right.

4 Clues Hinting at a Different Time (pairs)

There are many hints that 'Matilda' is not a contemporary poem. For example, her punishment for telling lies is to miss a trip to the theatre. Find other clues in the language and content which show that this is not a modern poem.

Language clues	Content clues
'Infirmity' means illness	*The fire brigade are described as galloping through the streets. This suggests that horses are pulling the . . .*

5 A Tragically Funny Poem (pairs)

How can the story of Matilda be sad and amusing at the same time? List all the things that make it a tragic poem, then list the amusing events and language. Which list is the most convincing?

Matilda Who Told Lies and Was Burned to Death

Matilda told such Dreadful Lies,
It made one Gasp and Stretch one's Eyes;
Her Aunt, who, from her Earliest Youth,
Had kept a Strict Regard for Truth,
Attempted to Believe Matilda: 5
The effort very nearly killed her,
And would have done so, had not She
Discovered this Infirmity.
For once, towards the Close of Day,
Matilda, growing tired of play,   10
And finding she was left alone,
Went tiptoe
        to
            the Telephone
And summoned the Immediate Aid   15
Of London's Noble Fire-Brigade.
Within an hour the Gallant Band
Were pouring in on every hand,
From Putney, Hackney Downs and Bow,
With Courage high and Hearts a-glow   20
They galloped, roaring through the Town,
'Matilda's House is Burning Down!'
Inspired by British Cheers and Loud
Proceeding from the Frenzied Crowd,
They ran their ladders through a score   25
Of windows on the Ball Room Floor;
And took Peculiar Pains to Souse
The pictures up and down the House,
Until Matilda's Aunt succeeded
In showing them they were not needed   30
And even then she had to pay
To get the Men to go away!

    * * *

It happened that a few Weeks later
Her Aunt was off to the Theatre
To see that Interesting Play   35
The Second Mrs Tanqueray.
She had refused to take her Niece
To hear this Entertaining Piece:
A Deprivation Just and Wise
To Punish her for Telling Lies.   40
That Night a Fire *did* break out –
You should have heard Matilda Shout!
You should have heard her Scream and Bawl,
And throw the window up and call
To people passing in the Street –   45
(The rapidly increasing Heat
Encouraging her to obtain
Their confidence) – but all in vain!
For every time she shouted 'Fire!'
They only answered 'Little Liar!'   50
And therefore when her Aunt returned,
Matilda, and the House, were Burned.

Hilaire Belloc

THE TICKING OF TIME

1 Time (pairs)

(a) What things last? Make a list of ten things that you think will survive three or four hundred years into the future.

(b) Use your notes to construct a poem. The first two lines explain what will be forgotten, the last two what will last through time. The opening four lines opposite might help you.

2 Timeline (pairs)

(a) Read the poem. It was written at the beginning of the seventeenth century and predicts what will disappear and what will survive.

(b) Construct a timeline illustrating and explaining Shakespeare's ideas so that they are clear to someone who hasn't read the poem.

1603	1793	18..
Shakespeare writes this poem. It is a 'powerful rime' which will . . .	However great and ornate a monument a prince builds to his memory, it will crumble. But the poem written opposite . . .	'Wasteful war shall . . .

3 Sonnets (pairs)

A *sonnet* is a fourteen-line poem with a structured rhyme scheme. Shakespeare's sonnets are structured like this:

quatrain 1	(4 lines)	a	b	a	b
quatrain 2	(4 lines)	c	d	c	d
quatrain 3	(4 lines)	e	f	e	f
couplet	(2 lines)	g	g		

Each quatrain is a unit of meaning. Read the poem carefully and label the sections with newspaper-style headlines like this:

Quatrain 2

PEN MORE POWERFUL THAN . . . . . .

Not Marble, Nor the Guilded Monument

Not marble, nor the guilded monument,
Of Princes shall out-live this powerfull rime,
But you shall shine more bright in these contents
Than unswept stone, besmeer'd with sluttish time.
When wastefull warre shall *Statues* over-turne,
And broiles roote out the worke of masonry,
Nor *Mars* his sword, nor warres quick fire shall burne
The living record of your memory.
Gainst death, and all oblivious enmity
Shall you pace forth, your praise shall stil finde roome,
Even in the eyes of all posterity
That weare this world out to the ending doome.
  So til the judgement that your selfe arise,
  You live in this, and dwell in lovers eies.

William Shakespeare

1 **Interrogating a Title (pairs)**

   (a) Titles are important because they give clues about a poem's content. What clues does the title 'His Poetrie His Pillar' give a reader?

   (b) Draw a detailed spider diagram which investigates this title.

   A pillar is used to . . .
   This suggests that . . .

His Poetrie
His Pillar

   'His' suggests . . .

   (c) Now read the poem. Can you add more to the spider diagram? What were some pillars used for in Herrick's time? And pyramids?

2 **The Poet versus the Cynic (two pairs)**

   In his poem Herrick argues that life is short. Lots of people die and 'lie forgot' (forgotten) in tombs and graves, but he will live on in his poetry. It is a monument that can't be removed.

   PAIR A
   Support Herrick's case that poetry lasts through time. You might like to consider that you are reading his ideas more than three hundred years after his death. Argue for the power of writing to influence people. Mention other writers who have made you, or others, rethink their opinions.

   PAIR B
   Prepare a case against Herrick. Talk about other people who lived in the past and are remembered. Argue that writing isn't important – who remembers words on a page?

   Once you have noted down your arguments, rehearse them separately. Then debate the issue.

His Poetrie His Pillar

Onely a little more
  I have to write,
  Then Ile give o're,
And bid the world Good-night.

'Tis but a flying minute,   5
  That I must stay,
  Or linger in it;
And then I must away.

O time that cut'st down all!
  And scarce leav'st here   10
  Memoriall
Of any men that were.

How many lye forgot
  In Vaults beneath?
  And piece-meale rot   15
Without a fame in death?

Behold this living stone,
  I reare for me,
  Ne'r to be thrown
Downe, envious Time by thee.   20

Pillars let some set up,
  (If so they please)
  Here is my hope,
And my *Pyramides*.

                    Robert Herrick

1 More Herrick Metaphors (pairs or individual work)

Robert Herrick describes how sad he is that the beautiful daffodils last such a short time. However, this poem uses metaphor to say something else at the same time.

Explore metaphors from the poem by using drawings and notes similar to this to explain them.

Faire Daffadills, we weep to see
You haste away so soone:

Daffodils (=beauty) die quickly
ie. beauty is short lived.

2 Changing the Beat and the Line Length (groups of three)

(a) Notice in the poem opposite that Herrick changes the length of his lines. Why are some lines shorter?

(b) Read the first verse out loud, counting the number of syllables in each line. Write these numbers down on a piece of paper. What is the effect of this difference in rhythm? Does it link to the meaning in any way? Would it make any difference if lines 5 and 6, and 7 and 8, were written in two lines not four?

(c) Write a parody or joke version of Herrick's poem. It should mirror his use of rhyme and rhythm, but change the subject of the poem. Here is the start of one student's version:

> *Sad chemistry, I'm glad to see*
> *You haste away so soon*

(d) Write an explanation about how your poem mirrors the style of Herrick's. There are notes on literary techniques to help you on page 128.

3 Mr Depressing

If you look at these two poems by Herrick you will see that they both talk about how short life is. Write a letter to Herrick which argues with his point of view.

To Daffadills

Faire Daffadills, we weep to see
    You haste away so soone:
As yet the early-rising Sun
    Has not attain'd his Noone.
Stay, stay,   5
        Untill the hasting day
Has run
        But to the Even-song;
And, having pray'd together, we
Will goe with you along.   10

We have short time to stay, as you,
    We have as short a Spring;

As quick a growth to meet Decay,
    As you, or any thing.
        We die,   15
        As your hours doe, and drie
                Away,
        Like to the Summers raine;
Or as the pearles of Mornings dew
        Ne'r to be found againe.   20

                    Robert Herrick

1 Round the Clock

(a) Copy this clock diagram. Notice how the hands point to ideas of what time means to some people. Fill in at least four other ideas.

(b) Draw a similar diagram to explore whether the moon can mean different things to different people.

2 Metaphors and Similes (groups of three)

We all use metaphors and similes to make comparisons. For example, in 'Time' Shelley compares time to the sea, and in 'The Moon' he uses a simile comparing the moon to a pale, dying lady. These illustrations show some of the comparisons Shelley makes. Work together to complete the picture.

3 Having a Nice Time

Shelley's poem describes the unpleasant things time brings: the tears, death, and terrible events.

List all the pleasant things you associate with time. Then copy out the title and opening lines of Shelley's poem as far as the word 'deep'. Develop this opening into a happy poem about the good things time brings.

Unfathomable Sea!

whose waves are years,

Ocean of Time,

whose waters of deep woe

Time

Unfathomable Sea! whose waves are years,
   Ocean of Time, whose waters of deep woe
Are brackish with the salt of human tears!
   Thou shoreless flood, which in thy ebb and flow
Claspest the limits of mortality,
And sick of prey, yet howling on for more,
Vomitest thy wrecks on its inhospitable shore;
   Treacherous in calm, and terrible in storm,
      Who shall put forth on thee,
      Unfathomable Sea?

Percy Bysshe Shelley

The Moon

And, like a dying lady lean and pale,
Who totters forth, wrapp'd in a gauzy veil,
Out of her chamber, led by the insane
And feeble wanderings of her fading brain,
The moon arose up in the murky east
A white and shapeless mass.

Art thou pale for weariness
Of climbing heaven and gazing on the earth,
Wandering companionless
Among the stars that have a different birth,
And ever changing, like a joyless eye
That finds no object worth its constancy?

Percy Bysshe Shelley

1 The Picture (pairs)

Imagine you travel to an old and mysterious country far away from home. Whilst there you stumble across a strange sight in the middle of the desert. A drawing of this scene is on the opposite page. Look carefully at it, discuss what it shows about the place, its ruler, what his people thought about him.

Note down your ideas in the form of a chart for display. Here is a start:

The place
Sand, desert. It looks bleak.
All that is left there . . .

The statue
The face of the statue looks . . .

YOUR IMPRESSIONS

**What his people
thought of Ozymandias**
Disliked. We can
tell this because . . .

The ruler
Called _____.
He believed he was a
mighty king.
Conceited – we know this
because . . .

CONTINUED ☞

2 The Word Picture (groups of three)

On the previous page you predicted what Ozymandias was like and how he treated his people. Here the poet considers this man who thought he was the king of kings.

(a) Divide the poem into three voices and read it aloud several times.

(b) Look back to your prediction diagram. What can you add to it? How did Ozymandias treat his people? What defeated him?

(c) Imagine you are one of Ozymandias's subjects. Write a diary entry about the day the statue was finished. Include a description of the statue and your opinions of your ruler.

3 Irony (pairs)

Irony is language with double meaning. It is used to add an alternative – and sometimes mocking – second meaning to the words.

Read lines 10–14 aloud. Write an explanation about how the inscription on Ozymandias's statue is ironic. Are there other ironies, or mocking double meanings, in the poem?

4 Postcards from the Desert

Postcards provide two pictures of a place: on one side is a visual image, and on the other the writer's words tell you about the scene.

Create your own postcard of the land of Ozymandias. On one side draw a vivid picture of the desert and the statue. On the reverse describe the statue, and say what you think of Ozymandias and his opinions.

5 Same Poet, Similar Message (pairs)

Both 'Ozymandias' and 'Time' (page 95) explore the theme of time. Write brief headlines which explain what Shelley is saying about time in each poem. Here is an example:

Ozymandias: Time will Beat You in the End

Then make your headlines into paragraphs which explain how Shelley describes time in these two poems. Use quotations from both poems to support your ideas.

Ozymandias

I met a traveller from an antique land
Who said: Two vast and trunkless legs of stone
Stand in the desert . . . Near them, on the sand,
Half sunk, a shattered visage lies, whose frown,
And wrinkled lip, and sneer of cold command,
Tell that its sculptor well those passions read
Which yet survive, stamped on these lifeless things,
The hand that mocked them, and the heart that fed:
And on the pedestal these words appear:
'My name is Ozymandias, king of kings:
Look on my works, ye Mighty, and despair!'
Nothing beside remains. Round the decay
Of that colossal wreck, boundless and bare
The lone and level sands stretch far away.

Percy Bysshe Shelley

1 The Wise Old Man (pairs roleplay)

One of you is a kindly wizard who understands the answers to most things. The other is a small child. The kind wizard finds the child in a small grove of trees. It is autumn, and beautiful golden leaves are tumbling to the ground. The child looks at the leaves and weeps but does not know why.

Devise a thirty-second roleplay in which the wizard finds the child and works out a reason for her tears. The final sentence in your roleplay should be a clear explanation from the wizard about why the child is crying.

2 Performance Read or Explanation (groups of four)

GROUP A

Prepare a reading of the poem which emphasises how the poem works. Try some of the following:

- Hand over to different readers at each punctuation mark.
- Emphasise the rhyme (it lies within the same line sometimes) and the rhythm.
- Show the alliteration.

GROUP B

Some of the words in the poem are deliberately disrupted, moved to a place where they seem out of order. For example, 'can you' at the end of line 4 would normally come earlier in a sentence or line. Where?
Find several examples of this disrupted word order. Explain and present them to the class.

At the end of your presentations, write two paragraphs about:

- what the poem is about
- the techniques Hopkins uses to express his ideas, and their effect.

3 'Spring and Fall' – the Cartoon Story

You are a cartoonist and have the job of telling the story of 'Spring and Fall' to 8 year olds. Use a combination of cartoon skills, Hopkins' language, and explanation.

Margaret, are you grieving over Goldengrove unleaving?

Spring and Fall

to a young child

Márgarét, áre you gríeving
Over Goldengrove unleaving?
Leáves líke the things of man, you
With your fresh thoughts care for, can you?
Ah! ás the heart grows older
It will come to such sights colder
By and by, nor spare a sigh
Though worlds of wanwood leafmeal lie;
And yet you will weep and know why.
Now no matter, child, the name:
Sórrow's spríngs áre the same.
Nor mouth had, no nor mind, expressed
What heart heard of, ghost guessed:
It ís the blight man was born for,
It is Margaret you mourn for.

Gerard Manley Hopkins

1 Reply to the Yellow-billed Alarm Clock (pairs)

Read 'Time to Rise' using both voices – the narrator and the bird.

Write 'sleepy-head's' reply to the bird using the same rhyme scheme and metre (rhythm) as the original verse. Use this as an opening line if you wish, or be more inventive:

This did the sleepy-head reply...

2 Comparing Poems (pairs or groups of three)

Both poems are written by Robert Louis Stevenson. Can you see similarities between them? Make notes comparing the poems. Use these headings:

	'Time to Rise'	'Winter Time'
Content: *what the poems are about*	*A sleepy person is reminded that...*	*Also describes someone rising from bed in a morning, but most of the poem focuses on...*
Language: *complex? simple? metaphor? Examples of dialect?*		
Form or structure: *verses, rhyme scheme, rhythm*		

Then write a short essay comparing the two poems.

3 My Wintry Response

Stevenson discusses how getting up, particularly on winter mornings, is difficult. Note down your ideas on getting up on a cold day.

Actions
Shiver in the chill
Huddle under...

Weather
Frosty, clear air
Jack Frost on...

RISING IN WINTER

Sounds
Distant rumble of traffic...

Feelings
Reluctant to...

Use this plan to draft a poem called 'Rising in Winter'.

Time to Rise

A birdie with a yellow bill
Hopped upon the window sill,
Cocked his shining eye and said:
'Ain't you 'shamed, you sleepy-head?'

Winter Time

Late lies the wintry sun a-bed,
A frosty, fiery sleepy-head;
Blinks but an hour or two; and then,
A blood-red orange, sets again.

Before the stars have left the skies,
At morning in the dark I rise;
And shivering in my nakedness,
By the cold candle, bathe and dress.

Robert Louis Stevenson

THE RIME OF THE ANCIENT MARINER

Preparation (groups of four)

'The Rime of the Ancient Mariner' is a long narrative poem telling a dramatic story. These pictures give clues about the events which take place.

(a) Decide on the order you think the pictures go in.

(b) Decide what story the pictures tell and perform it for the class.

Part 1

1 Mariner, Wedding-Guest and Company (groups of about six)

'The Rime of the Ancient Mariner' begins with a dramatic meeting. A wedding-guest is approached by an old sailor and told a strange story full of mystery and power . . .

Read Part 1 aloud, changing readers at each set of speech marks. After the reading, in your group retell the story as dramatically and in as much detail as possible.

2 The Power of the Mariner (pairs)

Make a list of all the lines and phrases in the poem which suggest that the Mariner holds a strange power over the Wedding-Guest. Add notes to your list which show what it is about him that is so powerful – his appearance, words, physical force . . .

Imagine you are the Wedding-Guest. Explain how the Mariner stopped you and what it was about him that made you sit and listen. You might begin:

I was on my way to a wedding with two friends when an old sailor approached me. I remember his long, flowing grey beard, but most of all I was struck by a peculiar glint in his eyes . . .

3 The Captain's Log (groups of three)

Each day the captain of a ship notes down significant events and changes in the weather. Begin at line 25 and jot down the notes the ship's captain might have made about this sea journey. This may help you begin:

> *Invent a date.*
> *Good start to voyage.*
> *Fair weather.*
> *Hot and burning sun regularly circled the ship . . .*

Use these notes to draft a full version of 'The Captain's Log'.

The Rime of the Ancient Mariner

Part 1

It is an ancient Mariner,
And he stoppeth one of three.
'By thy long grey beard and glittering eye,
Now wherefore stopp'st thou me?

The Bridegroom's doors are opened wide,   5
And I am next of kin;
The guests are met, the feast is set:
May'st hear the merry din.'

He holds him with his skinny hand,
'There was a ship,' quoth he.   10
'Hold off! unhand me, grey-beard loon!'
Eftsoons his hand dropt he.

He holds him with his glittering eye –
The Wedding-Guest stood still,
And listens like a three years' child: 15
The Mariner hath his will.

The Wedding-Guest sat on a stone:
He cannot choose but hear;
And thus spake on that ancient man,
The bright-eyed Mariner.   20

'The ship was cheered, the harbour cleared,
Merrily did we drop
Below the kirk, below the hill,
Below the lighthouse top.

The Sun came up upon the left,   25
Out of the sea came he!
And he shone bright, and on the right
Went down into the sea.

Higher and higher every day,
Till over the mast at noon –'   30
The Wedding-Guest here beat his breast,
For he heard the loud bassoon.

The bride hath paced into the hall,
Red as a rose is she;
Nodding their heads before her goes   35
The merry minstrelsy.

The Wedding-Guest he beat his breast,
Yet he cannot choose but hear;
And thus spake on that ancient man,
The bright-eyed Mariner.   40

'And now the Storm-blast came, and he
Was tyrannous and strong:
He struck with his o'ertaking wings,
And chased us south along.

With sloping masts and dipping prow,   45
As who pursued with yell and blow
Still treads the shadow of his foe,
And forward bends his head,
The ship drove fast, loud roared the blast,
And southward aye we fled.   50

And now there came both mist and snow,
And it grew wondrous cold:
And ice, mast-high, came floating by,
As green as emerald.

And through the drifts the snowy clifts   55
Did send a dismal sheen:
Nor shapes of men nor beasts we ken –
The ice was all between.

The ice was here, the ice was there,
The ice was all around: 60
It cracked and growled, and roared and howled,
Like noises in a swound!

At length did cross an Albatross,
Through the fog it came;
As if it had been a Christian soul,   65
We hailed it in God's name.

It ate the food it ne'er had eat,
And round and round it flew.
The ice did split with a thunder-fit;
The helmsman steered us through!   70

And a good south wind sprung up behind;
The Albatross did follow,
And every day, for food or play,
Came to the mariners' hollo!

CONTINUED ☞

Part 2

1 Mystic Mariners (groups of three or four)

The Mariner has just shot dead the bird which followed the ship and brought 'the good south wind' to its sails.

Imagine one of you is the killer of the bird, the others are fellow mariners. Improvise a scene on board the ship where the mariners accuse the murderer and predict what will happen now the bird is dead. How should the killer be punished?

Perform your drama for the class. Then read aloud Part 2 of the poem to see if you imagined the scene as Coleridge did.

2 A Painted Ship upon a Painted Ocean (groups of three)

Coleridge describes the silent sea and the slimy creatures that inhabit it. Prepare a list of descriptive phrases from line 111 onwards.

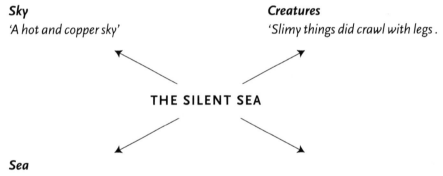

Sky
'A hot and copper sky'

Creatures
'Slimy things did crawl with legs .

THE SILENT SEA

Sea
'Like a witch's oils'

Add adjectives, descriptions and sketches of your own to the list.

3 Display Work (groups of three)

Prepare a group display for the classroom. This display should include the following:

(a) Two labelled pictures of The Silent Sea – one of a daytime scene with the sun at its height, the other at night as the death fires dance.

(b) Two prose descriptions of The Silent Sea, the first describing the sea by day, the second at night. Try to use short, shocking sentences to balance longer descriptive ones.

(c) A short poem describing this dreadful, silent sea.

Your work for activity 2 should give ideas on what to draw and write.

In mist or cloud, on mast or shroud,   75
It perched for vespers nine;
Whiles all the night, through fog-smoke white,
Glimmered the white Moon-shine.'

'God save thee, ancient Mariner!
From the fiends, that plague thee thus! –   80
Why look'st thou so?' – With my cross-bow
I shot the Albatross.

Part 2

The Sun now rose upon the right:
Out of the sea came he,
Still hid in mist, and on the left   85
Went down into the sea.

And the good south wind still blew behind,
But no sweet bird did follow,
Nor any day for food or play
Came to the mariners' hollo!   90

And I had done a hellish thing,
And it would work 'em woe:
For all averred, I had killed the bird
That made the breeze to blow.
Ah wretch! said they, the bird to slay,   95
That made the breeze to blow!

Nor dim nor red, like God's own head,
The glorious Sun uprist:
Then all averred, I had killed the bird
That brought the fog and mist.   100
'Twas right, said they, such birds to slay,
That bring the fog and mist.

The fair breeze blew, the white foam flew,
The furrow followed free;
We were the first that ever burst   105
Into that silent sea.

Down dropt the breeze, the sails dropt down,
'Twas sad as sad could be;
And we did speak only to break
The silence of the sea!   110

All in a hot and copper sky,
The bloody Sun, at noon,
Right up above the mast did stand,
No bigger than the Moon.

Day after day, day after day,   115
We stuck, nor breath nor motion;
As idle as a painted ship
Upon a painted ocean.

Water, water, every where,
And all the boards did shrink;   120
Water, water, every where,
Nor any drop to drink.

The very deep did rot: O Christ!
That ever this should be!
Yea, slimy things did crawl with legs   125
Upon the slimy sea.

About, about, in reel and rout
The death-fires danced at night;
The water, like a witch's oils,
Burnt green, and blue and white.   130

And some in dreams assuréd were
Of the Spirit that plagued us so;
Nine fathom deep he had followed us
From the land of mist and snow.

And every tongue, through utter drought,   135
Was withered at the root;
We could not speak, no more than if
We had been choked with soot.

Ah! well a-day! what evil looks
Had I from old and young!   140
Instead of the cross, the Albatross
About my neck was hung.

CONTINUED ☞

Part 3

1 Picture This (groups of four)

At the last stage of the Ancient Mariner's tale the crew were becalmed on the silent sea, dying slowly from thirst. The pictures below tell the next stages of the story.

Use the pictures to tell your version of the story.

Read the events opposite and see if you were right.

- Write captions for each picture using a combination of Coleridge's verse and your own ideas.
- Coleridge describes Death and his dreadful female companion playing dice. Who wins? How many die as a result of this victory? What is the last thing each dying man does?

Part 3

There passed a weary time. Each throat
Was parched, and glazed each eye.
A weary time! a weary time! 145
How glazed each weary eye,
When looking westward, I beheld
A something in the sky.

At first it seemed a little speck,
And then it seemed a mist; 150
It moved and moved, and took at last
A certain shape, I wist.

A speck, a mist, a shape, I wist!
And still it neared and neared:
As if it dodged a water-sprite, 155
It plunged and tacked and veered.

With throats unslaked, with black lips baked,
We could nor laugh nor wail;
Through utter drought all dumb we stood!
I bit my arm, I sucked the blood, 160
And cried, A sail! a sail!

With throats unslaked, with black lips baked,
Agape they heard me call:
Gramercy! they for joy did grin,
And all at once their breath drew in, 165
As they were drinking all.

See! see! (I cried) she tacks no more!
Hither to work us weal;
Without a breeze, without a tide,
She steadies with upright keel! 170

The western wave was all a-flame.
The day was well nigh done!
Almost upon the western wave
Rested the broad bright Sun;
When that strange shape drove suddenly 175
Betwixt us and the Sun.

And straight the Sun was flecked with bars,
(Heaven's Mother send us grace!)
As if through a dungeon-grate he peered
With broad and burning face. 180

Alas! (thought I, and my heart beat loud)
How fast she nears and nears!
Are those *her* sails that glance in the Sun,
Like restless gossameres?

Are those *her* ribs through which the Sun 185
Did peer, as through a grate?
And is that Woman all her crew?
Is that a Death? and are there two?
Is Death that woman's mate?

Her lips were red, *her* looks were free, 190
Her locks were yellow as gold:
Her skin was as white as leprosy,
The Night-mare Life-in-Death was she,
Who thicks man's blood with cold.

The naked hulk alongside came, 195
And the twain were casting dice;
'The game is done! I've won! I've won!'
Quoth she, and whistles thrice.

The Sun's rim dips; the stars rush out:
At one stride comes the dark; 200
With far-heard whisper, o'er the sea,
Off shot the spectre-bark.

We listened and looked sideways up!
Fear at my heart, as at a cup,
My life-blood seemed to sip! 205
The stars were dim, and thick the night,
The steersman's face by his lamp gleamed
     white;
From the sails the dew did drip –

Till clombe above the eastern bar
The hornéd Moon, with one bright star 210
Within the nether tip.

One after one, by the star-dogged Moon,
Too quick for groan or sigh,
Each turned his face with a ghastly pang,
And cursed me with his eye. 215

Four times fifty living men,
(And I heard nor sigh nor groan)
With heavy thump, a lifeless lump,
They dropped down one by one.

The souls did from their bodies fly – 220
They fled to bliss or woe!
And every soul, it passed me by,
Like the whizz of my cross-bow!

CONTINUED ☞

Part 4

1 Real or Symbolic? (pairs)

In lines 139–142 the Albatross is hung around the neck of the Ancient
Mariner. In lines 272–291 the bird falls from his neck and sinks into the
sea. Was a real bird tied round his neck all this time, or is the bird symbolic,
representing something else?

Write a 'Real or Symbolic' chart exploring what Coleridge's bird might be.

2 Why So Afraid? (groups of four)

Part 4 begins with the Wedding-Guest exclaiming that he is afraid of the
Mariner. Lines 224–231 give three reasons for his terror.

(a) Perform the lines using the actions and voices of the Wedding-Guest
and Mariner.

(b) Decide on three possible reasons for the Wedding-Guest's fear, and
list these in rank order.

3 The Nightmare Life-in-Death (pairs)

Lines 190–198 tell how the nightmare Life-in-Death played dice to win the
souls of the mariners. In what ways is the surviving mariner's existence a
living nightmare, a living death?

(a) Continue this table to explain the horror of the Mariner's existence:

Living Death Explanations of how the Mariner is enduring a fate worse than death	Language Words that show the horror of his situation
He is totally alone. No one to help or take pity on him. He feels he can't be forgiven for . . .	Repetition of 'alone' shows . . . Long, drawn-out sound of the word '_____' (line 232) shows . . .
He is living amongst . . .	Use of alliteration

Part 4

'I fear thee, ancient Mariner!
I fear thy skinny hand!   225
And thou art long, and lank, and brown,
As is the ribbed sea-sand.

I fear thee and thy glittering eye,
And thy skinny hand, so brown.' –
Fear not, fear not, thou Wedding-Guest!   230
This body dropt not down.

Alone, alone, all, all alone,
Alone on a wide wide sea!
And never a saint took pity on
My soul in agony.   235

The many men, so beautiful!
And they all dead did lie:
And a thousand thousand slimy things
Lived on; and so did I.

I looked upon the rotting sea,   240
And drew my eyes away;
I looked upon the rotting deck,
And there the dead men lay.

I looked to heaven, and tried to pray;
But or ever a prayer had gusht,   245
A wicked whisper came, and made
My heart as dry as dust.

I closed my lids, and kept them close,
And the balls like pulses beat;
For the sky and the sea, and the sea and
   the sky   250
Lay like a load on my weary eye,
And the dead were at my feet.

The cold sweat melted from their limbs,
Nor rot nor reek did they:
The look with which they looked on me   255
Had never passed away.

CONTINUED ☞

(b) Write a literary critical essay in response to the following: 'Describe the Ancient Mariner's living death and how Coleridge's language makes us experience his pain.'

You will find an example of a plan for a literary critical essay on page 128 which will help you. Here is the start of an essay plan by a student.

The first paragraph
Include the title of the poem and the poet. Write a brief explanation of what the Mariner has done and how he is suffering now for this. Explain how he is enduring a kind of living death. Explain 'living death' and explore how Coleridge's use of language techniques heightens our awareness of the Mariner's suffering.

Work with a partner to draft this first paragraph. Remember: an introduction to an essay is usually short (no more than ten lines). Read your opening aloud to the class and listen to other examples; adapt and change yours.

Now plan the rest of the essay before writing it (the chart you wrote earlier should help you). This picture plan may help too.

guilt

re-lives experience

LIFE IN DEATH

isolated

surrounded by . . .

An orphan's curse would drag to hell
A spirit from on high;
But oh! more horrible than that
Is the curse in a dead man's eye!   260
Seven days, seven nights, I saw that curse,
And yet I could not die.

The moving Moon went up the sky,
And no where did abide:
Softly she was going up,   265
And a star or two beside –

Her beams bemocked the sultry main,
Like April hoar-frost spread;
But where the ship's huge shadow lay,
The charméd water burnt alway   270
A still and awful red.

Beyond the shadow of the ship,
I watched the water-snakes:
They moved in tracks of shining white,
And when they reared, the elfish light   275
Fell off in hoary flakes.

Within the shadow of the ship
I watched their rich attire:
Blue, glossy green, and velvet black,
They coiled and swam; and every track   280
Was a flash of golden fire.

O happy living things! no tongue
Their beauty might declare:
A spring of love gushed from my heart,
And I blessed them unaware: 285
Sure my kind saint took pity on me,
And I blessed them unaware.

The self-same moment I could pray;
And from my neck so free
The Albatross fell off, and sank   290
Like lead into the sea.

CONTINUED ☞

Part 5

1 The Raising of the Dead (groups of six or eight)

Lines 329–362 describe how the dead mariners arise, but they are not as
frightening as the Wedding-Guest first believes them to be.

Read this section aloud as a group, then work out a performance of these
lines with narrators, mariners, the spirit of the Mariner's nephew and the
Wedding-Guest. Learn your lines and perform this section for the class.

2 Language Work (pairs)

Many words in this poem are unfamiliar today but can be worked out from
the context.

Write down every unfamiliar word in this section of the poem and guess at
its meaning, then go on and check if you were right by using a dictionary.

Make a glossary of 'Ancient Mariner' words for the poem so far. Here is an
example of one section of a page:

Ancient Mariner glossary		
line 310	'anear'	close by or near – the wind did not come near the Mariner
line 314	'a hundred fire-flags sheen'	a hundred fire-flags shone Fire-flags are now called . . .
line 319	'sedge'	a grass-like plant with triangular (sail-like) leaves

Part 5

Oh sleep! it is a gentle thing,
Beloved from pole to pole!
To Mary Queen the praise be given!
She sent the gentle sleep from Heaven,   295
That slid into my soul.

The silly buckets on the deck,
That had so long remained,
I dreamt that they were filled with dew;
And when I awoke, it rained.   300

My lips were wet, my throat was cold,
My garments all were dank;
Sure I had drunken in my dreams,
And still my body drank.

I moved, and could not feel my limbs: 305
I was so light – almost
I thought that I had died in sleep,
And was a blessèd ghost.

And soon I heard a roaring wind:
It did not come anear;   310
But with its sound it shook the sails,
That were so thin and sere.

The upper air burst into life!
And a hundred fire-flags sheen,
To and fro they were hurried about!   315
And to and fro, and in and out,
The wan stars danced between.

And the coming wind did roar more loud,
And the sails did sigh like sedge;
And the rain poured down from one black
    cloud;   320
The Moon was at its edge.

The thick black cloud was cleft, and still
The Moon was at its side:
Like waters shot from some high crag,
The lightning fell with never a jag,   325
A river steep and wide.

The loud wind never reached the ship,
Yet now the ship moved on!
Beneath the lightning and the Moon
The dead men gave a groan.   330

They groaned, they stirred, they all uprose,
Nor spake, nor moved their eyes;
It had been strange, even in a dream,
To have seen those dead men rise.

The helmsman steered, the ship moved on;   335
Yet never a breeze up-blew;
The mariners all 'gan work the ropes,
Where they were wont to do;
They raised their limbs like lifeless tools –
We were a ghastly crew.   340

The body of my brother's son
Stood by me, knee to knee:
The body and I pulled at one rope,
But he said nought to me.

'I fear thee, ancient Mariner!'   345
Be calm, thou Wedding-Guest!
'Twas not those souls that fled in pain,
Which to their corses came again,
But a troop of spirits blest:

For when it dawned – they dropped their arms,   350
And clustered round the mast;
Sweet sounds rose slowly through their mouths,
And from their bodies passed.

Around, around, flew each sweet sound,
Then darted to the Sun;   355
Slowly the sounds came back again,
Now mixed, now one by one.

Sometimes a-dropping from the sky
I heard the sky-lark sing;
Sometimes all little birds that are,   360
How they seemed to fill the sea and air
With their sweet jargoning!

CONTINUED ☞

3 Who Is He? (pairs)

The end of Part 5 describes how the Mariner 'fell down in a swound' (fainted). He then hears two voices, but the identity of the speakers is kept hidden.

Read lines 383–409 aloud, using two voices. Present your reading to the class and at the end explain to whom the voices belong.

4 'And Penance More Will Do' (pairs)

At the end of this section Coleridge suggests that the Mariner will have to suffer for his crime. What penance do you think the Mariner will have to do?

5 Write Another Verse (drafting in pairs)

In lines 377–382 Coleridge mentions the 'land of mist and snow'. Imagine what this region might look like and continue this diagram:

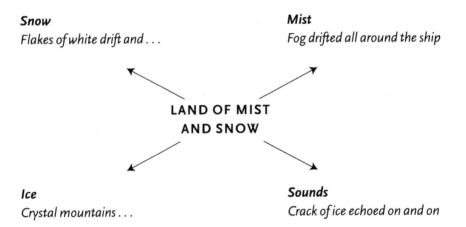

Snow
Flakes of white drift and . . .

Mist
Fog drifted all around the ship

LAND OF MIST AND SNOW

Ice
Crystal mountains . . .

Sounds
Crack of ice echoed on and on

Use this diagram as a basis for writing an additional six-line verse for 'The Ancient Mariner' which describes the land of mist and snow.

- Keep to the same a, b, c, b, d, b rhyme scheme as Coleridge.

- Try to keep to the same rhythm.

And now 'twas like all instruments,
Now like a lonely flute;
And now it is an angel's song,   365
That makes the heavens be mute.

It ceased; yet still the sails made on
A pleasant noise till noon,
A noise like of a hidden brook
In the leafy month of June,   370
That to the sleeping woods all night
Singeth a quiet tune.

Till noon we quietly sailed on,
Yet never a breeze did breathe:
Slowly and smoothly went the ship,   375
Moved onward from beneath.

Under the keel nine fathom deep,
From the land of mist and snow,
The spirit slid: and it was he
That made the ship to go.   380
The sails at noon left off their tune,
And the ship stood still also.

The Sun, right up above the mast,
Had fixed her to the ocean:
But in a minute she 'gan stir,   385
With a short uneasy motion –
Backwards and forwards half her length
With a short uneasy motion.

Then like a pawing horse let go,
She made a sudden bound: 390
It flung the blood into my head,
And I fell down in a swound.
How long in that same fit I lay,
I have not to declare;
But ere my living life returned,   395
I heard and in my soul discerned
Two voices in the air.

'Is it he?' quoth one, 'Is this the man?
By him who died on cross,
With his cruel bow he laid full low   400
The harmless Albatross.

The spirit who bideth by himself
In the land of mist and snow,
He loved the bird that loved the man
Who shot him with his bow.'   405

The other was a softer voice,
As soft as honey-dew:
Quoth he, 'The man hath penance done,
And penance more will do.'

CONTINUED ☞

Part 6

1 Influencing an Audience (pairs)

The way a story is told is sometimes as important as what it is about. A writer thinks about:

- *Form/genre*: whether to write a poem, prose, drama, horror, romance . . .
- *Tone*: the tone of voice to use–: witty, serious, warning, fearful . . . Is it spoken directly to you? Does the tone change?
- *Style*: how to tell the story–: choice of language, similes, rhythm, rhyme . . .

(a) Discuss the choices Coleridge made for each of the above.

(b) Much of 'The Ancient Mariner' is told in the first person ('I'). Read Part 6 of the poem and choose three or four verses from line 452 onwards to retell in the third person (he/she). For example, 451–459 might become:

A wind arose which fanned the Mariner's cheek and hair. He still felt afraid yet the wind also cheered his spirits and was welcome.

What is the effect of this change?

Part 6

FIRST VOICE

'But tell me, tell me! speak again,   410
Thy soft response renewing –
What makes that ship drive on so fast?
What is the ocean doing?'

SECOND VOICE

'Still as a slave before his lord,
The ocean hath no blast;   415
His great bright eye most silently
Up to the Moon is cast –

If he may know which way to go;
For she guides him smooth or grim.
See, brother, see! how graciously   420
She looketh down on him.'

FIRST VOICE

'But why drives on that ship so fast,
Without or wave or wind?'

SECOND VOICE

'The air is cut away before,
And closes from behind.   425

Fly, brother, fly! more high, more high!
Or we shall be belated:
For slow and slow that ship will go,
When the Mariner's trance is abated.'

I woke, and we were sailing on   430
As in a gentle weather:
'Twas night, calm night, the moon was high;
The dead men stood together.

All stood together on the deck,
For a charnel-dungeon fitter: 435
All fixed on me their stony eyes,
That in the Moon did glitter.

The pang, the curse, with which they died,
Had never passed away:
I could not draw my eyes from theirs,   440
Nor turn them up to pray.

And now this spell was snapt: once more
I viewed the ocean green,
And looked far forth, yet little saw
Of what had else been seen –   445

Like one, that on a lonesome road
Doth walk in fear and dread,
And having once turned round walks on,
And turns no more his head;
Because he knows, a frightful fiend   450
Doth close behind him tread.

But soon there breathed a wind on me,
Nor sound nor motion made:
Its path was not upon the sea,
In ripple or in shade.   455

It raised my hair, it fanned my cheek
Like a meadow-gale of spring –
It mingled strangely with my fears,
Yet it felt like a welcoming.

Swiftly, swiftly flew the ship,   460
Yet she sailed softly too:
Sweetly, sweetly blew the breeze –
On me alone it blew.

CONTINUED ☞

2 Influencing an Audience: Drama Script (groups of three)

A twentieth-century writer, Michael Bogdanov, turned Coleridge's poem into a drama script with two main characters: Young Mariner and Ancient Mariner. Read or perform the extract below.

The image of the shoreline is silhouetted on the sail, and the warning bell is heard. The Young Mariner climbs the rigging to look out.

YOUNG MARINER   Oh dream of joy! is this indeed
                       The light-house top I see?
                       Is this the hill? Is this the kirk?
                       Is this mine own countree?

ANCIENT MARINER   The harbour-bay was clear as glass,
                       So smoothly it was strewn!
                       And on the bay the moonlight lay,
                       And the shadow of the moon.

                       And the bay was white with silent light,
                       Till rising from the same,
                       Full many shapes, that shadows were,
                       In crimson colours came.

Red ribbons rise from the floor stage left and right. The deck is bathed in blood-red light.

YOUNG MARINER   Oh, Christ! what saw I there?

ANCIENT MARINER   Each corse lay flat, lifeless and flat.

Bogdanov adapted the poem by editing lines and adding stage directions to show actions. He also added extra characters.

(a) Continue a script like this from line 488 to the end of the poem.

(b) What is the effect of changing the form to a drama? Do you also have to adapt tone and language?

Oh! dream of joy! is this indeed
The light-house top I see?   465
Is this the hill? is this the kirk?
Is this mine own countree?

We drifted o'er the harbour-bar,
And I with sobs did pray –
O let me be awake, my God!   470
Or let me sleep alway.

The harbour-bay was clear as glass,
So smoothly it was strewn!
And on the bay the moonlight lay,
And the shadow of the Moon.   475

The rock shone bright, the kirk no less,
That stands above the rock:
The moonlight steeped in silentness
The steady weathercock.

And the bay was white with silent light,   480
Till rising from the same,
Full many shapes, that shadows were,
In crimson colours came.

A little distance from the prow
Those crimson shadows were: 485
I turned my eyes upon the deck –
Oh, Christ! what saw I there!

Each corse lay flat, lifeless and flat,
And, by the holy rood!
A man all light, a seraph-man,   490
On every corse there stood.

This seraph-band, each waved his hand:
It was a heavenly sight!
They stood as signals to the land,
Each one a lovely light;   495

This seraph-band, each waved his hand,
No voice did they impart –
No voice; but oh! the silence sank
Like music on my heart.

But soon I heard the dash of oars,   500
I heard the Pilot's cheer;
My head was turned perforce away
And I saw a boat appear.

The Pilot and the Pilot's boy,
I heard them coming fast: 505
Dear Lord in Heaven! it was a joy
The dead men could not blast.

I saw a third – I heard his voice:
It is the Hermit good!
He singeth loud his godly hymns   510
That he makes in the wood.
He'll shrieve my soul, he'll wash away
The Albatross's blood.

CONTINUED ☞

Part 7

1 Why Tell the Tale? (pairs)

The Mariner returns to his own land and tells his story to the hermit (the holy man who usually lives in solitude), but he tells his tale more than once.

Read lines 574–590 and make notes on why the Mariner tells his tale so often. Why does Coleridge write (line 590) that the Mariner 'teach(es)' others? Is this a story with a moral? Use your notes to write a full answer.

2 Illustrated Versions (pairs)

'The Ancient Mariner' has inspired many artists: illustrations of the Mariner's tale can be seen on pages 104–105 and the Bogdanov drama script on page 122. It has been argued that this poem could also be adapted to make a comic strip. Below is one artist's idea.

Plan, write and illustrate a comic strip which tells the whole story.

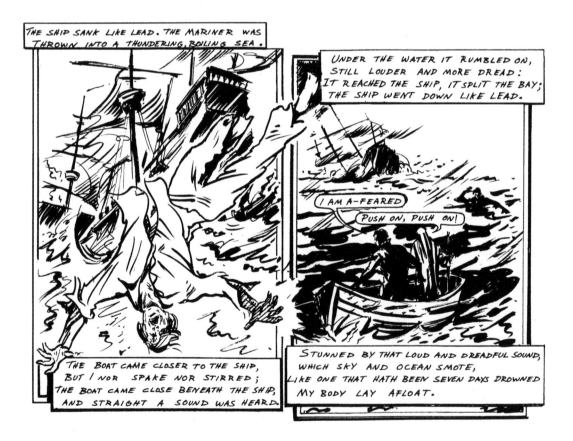

Part 7

This Hermit good lives in that wood
Which slopes down to the sea. 515
How loudly his sweet voice he rears!
He loves to talk with marineres
That come from a far countree.

He kneels at morn, and noon, and eve –
He hath a cushion plump: 520
It is the moss that wholly hides
The rotted old oak-stump.

The skiff-boat neared: I heard them talk,
'Why, this is strange, I trow!
Where are those lights so many and fair, 525
That signal made but now?'

'Strange, by my faith!' the Hermit said –
'And they answered not our cheer!
The planks looked warped! and see those sails,
How thin they are and sere! 530
I never saw aught like to them,
Unless perchance it were

Brown skeletons of leaves that lag
My forest-brook along;
When the ivy-tod is heavy with snow, 535
And the owlet whoops to the wolf below,
That eats the she-wolf's young.'

'Dear Lord! it hath a fiendish look –
(The Pilot made reply)
I am a-feared' – 'Push on, push on!' 540
Said the Hermit cheerily.

The boat came closer to the ship,
But I nor spake nor stirred;
The boat came close beneath the ship,
And straight a sound was heard. 545

Under the water it rumbled on,
Still louder and more dread:
It reached the ship, it split the bay;
The ship went down like lead.

Stunned by that loud and dreadful sound, 550
Which sky and ocean smote,
Like one that hath been seven days drowned
My body lay afloat;
But swift as dreams, myself I found
Within the Pilot's boat. 555

Upon the whirl, where sank the ship,
The boat spun round and round;
And all was still, save that the hill
Was telling of the sound.

I moved my lips – the Pilot shrieked 560
And fell down in a fit;
The holy Hermit raised his eyes,
And prayed where he did sit.

I took the oars: the Pilot's boy,
Who now doth crazy go, 565
Laughed loud and long, and all the while
His eyes went to and fro.
'Ha! ha!' quoth he, 'full plain I see,
The Devil knows how to row.'

And now, all in my own countree, 570
I stood on the firm land!
The Hermit stepped forth from the boat,
And scarcely he could stand.

'O shrieve me, shrieve me, holy man!'
The Hermit crossed his brow. 575
'Say quick,' quoth he, 'I bid thee say –
What manner of man art thou?'
Forthwith this frame of mine was wrenched
With a woful agony,
Which forced me to begin my tale; 580
And then it left me free.

Since then, at an uncertain hour,
That agony returns:
And till my ghastly tale is told,
This heart within me burns. 585

CONTINUED ☞

I pass, like night, from land to land;
I have strange power of speech;
That moment that his face I see,
I know the man that must hear me:
To him my tale I teach. 590

What loud uproar bursts from that door!
The wedding-guests are there:
But in the garden-bower the bride
And bride-maids singing are:
And hark the little vesper bell, 595
Which biddeth me to prayer!

O Wedding-Guest! this soul hath been
Alone on a wide wide sea:
So lonely 'twas, that God himself
Scarce seeméd there to be. 600

O sweeter than the marriage-feast,
'Tis sweeter far to me,
To walk together to the kirk
With a goodly company! –

To walk together to the kirk, 605
And all together pray,
While each to his great Father bends,
Old men, and babes, and loving friends
And youths and maidens gay!

Farewell, farewell! but this I tell 610
To thee, thou Wedding-Guest!
He prayeth well, who loveth well
Both man and bird and beast.

He prayeth best, who loveth best
All things both great and small; 615
For the dear God who loveth us,
He made and loveth all.

The Mariner, whose eye is bright,
Whose beard with age is hoar,
Is gone: and now the Wedding-Guest 620
Turned from the bridegroom's door.

He went like one that hath been stunned,
And is of sense forlorn:
A sadder and a wiser man,
He rose the morrow morn. 625

Samuel Taylor Coleridge

Looking back at 'The Rime of the Ancient Mariner'

1 What is the Poem About? (groups of three or four)

There are many different interpretations of the meaning of 'The Ancient Mariner'. Some say it is a straightforward adventure story with a naive young hero who needs to learn a lesson, while others feel it has religious meaning, or that it is a morality tale (a more serious version of 'Matilda' – see page 87).

Divide into groups to gather evidence for a particular view, then discuss what 'The Ancient Mariner' is about as a class.

> **Group A**   the poem is an adventure tale
> **Group B**   the poem has religious significance
> **Group C**   the poem is a morality tale

The following steps may help you:

- **Define your terms**
  A tale with religious significance, for example, must have elements or ideas which link to religion. For example what events in the poem might parallel the life of Christ.

- **Find evidence to support your ideas**
  If you are finding evidence to prove that the poem is an adventure tale, then look for key moments of drama and show how they are used as 'cliffhangers' to keep the listener interested.

- **Make links to other literature or stories**
  A morality tale shows someone making a mistake, paying for it and repenting. Show how other morality stories parallel 'The Ancient Mariner'.

2 The Mariner's Next Victim

Imagine you are the next person whom the Mariner stops. Write your experience as a poem. Explain where you were going, how you were approached and how you reacted. Try to use a similar style to Coleridge's – think about the use of rhyme, rhythm, alliteration and repetition.

3 Mariner Mini-saga

A *mini-saga* is a complete story told in few words. Can you tell the story of 'The Ancient Mariner' in 150 words?

4 Coleridge's Style (groups of three)

Writers use literary techniques to create certain effects and to influence the reader.

Coleridge uses many literary techniques in his poem. Copy and complete this table to keep a record of his style and its effects.

Technique used and definition	Examples	Effect
Alliteration: repetition of the same . . .	'The Wedding-Guest beat his breast.'	Creates a powerful sound which is similar to . . .
Repetition:		
Rhyme: (a) Internal rhyme when words on the same line rhyme (b) End rhyme when . . .		
Personification:	Lots of examples of the sun being personified . . .	
Rhythm and changes in rhythm:		

Use this as a plan from which to write an essay on Coleridge's use of language and its effects.

5 The Wedding-Guests Tells All (groups of five)

At the opening of the poem Coleridge describes how the Mariner stopped one of the three wedding-guests. Imagine that one or possibly two of the other guests hid and listened as well!

(a) Jot down the main events of the tale that the wedding-guests might remember.

(b) Use this list to present an improvisation where the guests go to the wedding and explain why they were late.

Printed in the United States
By Bookmasters